TWAYNE'S WORLD AUTHORS SERIES
A Survey of the World's Literature

Sylvia E. Bowman, Indiana University
GENERAL EDITOR

CANADA

Joseph Jones, University of Texas
EDITOR

James Reaney

(TWAS 49)

TWAYNE'S WORLD AUTHORS SERIES (TWAS)

The purpose of TWAS is to survey the major writers —novelists, dramatists, historians, poets, philosophers, and critics—of the nations of the world. Among the national literatures covered are those of Australia, Canada, China, Eastern Europe, France, Germany, Greece, India, Italy, Japan, Latin America, New Zealand, Poland, Russia, Scandinavia, Spain, and the African nations, as well as Hebrew, Yiddish, and Latin Classical literatures. This survey is complemented by Twayne's United States Authors Series and English Authors Series.

The intent of each volume in these series is to present a critical-analytical study of the works of the writer; to include biographical and historical material that may be necessary for understanding, appreciation, and critical appraisal of the writer; and to present all material in clear, concise English—but not to vitiate the scholarly content of the work by doing so.

James Reaney

By ALVIN A. LEE

McMaster University

Twayne Publishers, Inc.   ::   New York

To Hope, my wife

Preface

James Crerar Reaney, whose writings are the subject of this book, has for several years enjoyed recognition as one of the few most important poets currently active in Canada. Having staked a sure claim on the attention of the Canadian literary community while still a university undergraduate in the 'forties—with the publication of skillfully-written macabre short stories and a book of poems quite unlike anything else in Canadian poetry at the time—he has gone on to excel in several areas. He is above all a poet of extraordinary power, versatility, and craftsmanship. In addition, he is a university teacher, the editor of the influential little magazine *Alphabet,* a reviewer and critic, a creator of marionette shows, and, in recent years, a playwright beginning to attract international attention.

For obvious reasons this book is an interim report. Reaney is forty years old, at the height of his literary powers, and giving every indication of unabating creative activity. It may well be that his future work as poet and playwright, added to his present achievement, will show him to be a major literary figure. At the very least, his productions over the past twenty years command attention in a way that only a very few other writings in Canada do. They merit consideration in a frame of reference wider than that of Canadian literature, even though each of them grows from intensely localized experiences.

My purpose has been to describe and interpret Reaney's literary achievement so far, beginning with the early pieces and proceeding, not always chronologically, through the various texts which comprise his most important statements—pastoral, satiric, and comic—up to and including the year 1966. It has been possible to divide the considerable body of material involved into three significant groupings, indicated in the titles of the first three chapters, and determined by the main imaginative emphasis in each text. Certain important and very worthwhile single poems, however, like "The Dead Rainbow," "The Birth of Venus," and "The Tall Black Hat," although mentioned in the Bibliography, have not been discussed. Since space is limited in a study of this size, it has seemed advisable to concentrate, in the main, on the book-length productions and the plays, leaving the interested reader to use the Bibliography and search out further matter for himself. The good things slighted by this procedure, if included, would support, not undercut, the argument of the book. Several of the best of them, originally published more or less randomly in little magazines are now readily available in Milton Wilson's *Poetry of Mid-Century: 1940-1960* (New Canadian Library Original, 1964).

The early stories and poems, the poems in *The Red Heart* (1949), and the relatively late *Twelve Letters to a Small Town* (1962) have their main impetus in an intense desire to make literary sense out of a particular locale, by setting against its grotesque, destructive aspects a vision of what in one poem is called "pluperfect things"—the fleeting moments of happiness in the life of a marionette, an artifact of golden wallpaper, or the brief, precarious marriage of a lover-sun and a human heart. The *Letters* point to a perfection which is more secure than anything in the earlier pieces but they are also a recreation, in an idealized, simplified way, of a particular locale, not unlike that in the early poems "The School Globe" and "Gray Pillar." Similarly the dominantly satirical pieces—*A Suit of Nettles*, "A Message to Winnipeg," and *The Dance of Death at London, Ontario*—however complex they at times are, especially in the case of *A Suit of Nettles*, are Doomsday poems culminating in a vision of destruction and a wild *danse macabre*. The plays are grouped together not primarily for generic reasons, although this has its obvious advantages, but because the vision of reality which comes to dominate in them is one on the other side of Doomsday. In these the Red Heart is not annihilated nor left miserable in a sterile land; he is permitted to grow and take his place in an order of things in which the attainment of desire is possible. Even the dark comedy *One-man Masque*, which might equally well be included in Chapter Two, moves to this level of reality.

The handling of Reaney's writings in this way permits a fairly close reading of key texts, a recognition of each one's affinities with its closest relations, and a sense of certain basic early patterns receiving later elaboration. It also enables the reader not content with close reading to step back and observe the large structure or abstract design which identifies the particular group of works. Finally, in the last pages of the book, an attempt is made to describe Reaney's overall imaginative construct and to relate this to a mythopeic tradition in classical English poetry. The Bibliography lists all Reaney's numerous publications except reviews, as well as a few important items not yet in print. In addition it lists and annotates the relatively little critical writing on Reaney's work, most of this being simply in the form of reviews. These last have seemed worth including in a volume devoted to the study of a living, controversial writer whose reputation is in the process of being made.

This book has been completed with the generous help of James Reaney. By mutual consent we have left the task of critical interpretation to the present writer, but Mr. Reaney has provided unpublished manuscripts and has been most cooperative both in giving factual information and in reading the book in manuscript form. Also, to Mr. Reaney and to his agent, Sybil Hutchinson, my thanks for permission to quote from *The Red Heart*.

Jay Macpherson and Milton Wilson have read the manuscript. My sincere thanks to both, for their encouragement and useful comments.

In addition I wish to express gratitude to the following publishers:

Canadian Literature, for permission to use material from my article, "A Turn to the Stage: Reaney's Dramatic Verse" (numbers 15 & 16, Winter & Spring, 1963).

Macmillan of Canada, for permission to quote from *A Suit of Nettles* (1958) and from *The Killdeer & other Plays* (1962).

The Ryerson Press, for permission to quote from *Twelve Letters to a Small Town* (1962).

Finally, I wish to thank McMaster University for their support in the completion of this book.

ALVIN LEE

McMaster University

Contents

Chronology

1926   James Crerar Reaney born near Stratford, Ontario, to
        James Nesbitt Reaney and Elizabeth Henrietta Reaney
        (née Crerar). Half brother Ronald and half sister Wilma,
        both younger.

1932–   Attended Elmhurst public school, U. S. S. Number 9,
1939   South Easthope.

1939–   Attended Stratford Collegiate and Vocational Institute.
1944

1944–   Studied English Language and Literature at University
1948   College in the University of Toronto. Wrote poems and
        short stories; published in *Canadian Poetry Magazine,*
        Candian Forum, Contemporary Verse, Driftwind, Here
        and Now, Northern Review, and *The Undergrad.* Epstein
        award for short story and poetry writing.

1949   *The Red Heart* published. Won the Governor General's
        Award for the best volume of poetry published in 1949.
        Received M. A. degree in English from the University of
        Toronto.

1949–   Member of the Department of English in the University
1956   of Manitoba. Published in *Canadian Forum, Queen's*
        Quarterly, and *Contemporary Verse.* In December, 1951
        married Colleen Thibaudeau, herself a poet. A son, James
        Stewart, born 1952. A second son, John Andrew, born
        1954.

1956–   Advisory editor for *Tamarack Review.*
1960

1956–   A doctoral candidate in English in the School of Graduate
1958   Studies of the University of Toronto. President of the
        Graduate English Club. Wrote and produced a satirical
        play about the Ph.D. examinations, *From "Beowulf" to*
        Virginia Woolf. Doctoral dissertation, "The Influence of

Spenser on Yeats," supervised by Northrop Frye; received the degree 1958. Wrote (1956-1957) and published (1958) *A Suit of Nettles;* won the Governor General's Award for the best volume of poetry in 1958.

1958 Wrote *The Sun and the Moon* and entered it in the *Globe and Mail*-sponsored playwriting competition for the Stratford Shakespearean Festival.

1958– Resumed his position at the University of Manitoba.
1960

1959 *Night-blooming Cereus* performed on "CBC Wednesday Night," March 4. Studied typesetting in anticipation of publishing *Alphabet*. Wrote *The Killdeer* during the summer. A daughter, Susan Alice Elizabeth, born.

1960 *The Killdeer* performed by the University Alumnae Dramatic Club, directed by Pamela Terry, at the Coach House Theatre, Toronto, beginning January 13; *The Killdeer* entered in the annual Dominion Drama Festival and performed three times in Hart House Theatre, Toronto, and again in the Queen Elizabeth Auditorium, Vancouver. *Night-blooming Cereus* repeated on "CBC Wednesday Night." *One-man Masque* (acted by Reaney) and *Night-blooming Cereus* performed as a double bill in Hart House Theatre, April 6-7. Accepted position in the Department of English of Middlesex College in the University of Western Ontario, London. First issue of *Alphabet* published in September.

1961 *One-man Masque* performed by Jeremy Wilkin on CBC Television's "Q for Quest" in January. *The Killdeer,* starring Don Bryn, Kate Reid, Amelia Hall, and Robin Gammell, performed on CBC Television's "Festival 61" in June. Adapted Cyril Tourneur's *The Revenger's Tragedie* for "CBC Wednesday Night"; not produced. *Twelve Letters to a Small Town* performed on "CBC Wednesday Night" in July.

1962 *The Easter Egg* given a rehearsed reading at the University of Western Ontario on March 2; premiere performance by the University Alumnae Dramatic Club at McMaster University's first Festival of the Arts, in Hamilton, Ontario, on November 2, followed by ten performances at the Coach House Theatre in Toronto; still unpublished. *The Killdeer & other Plays* published; won the Governor General's Award for the best drama published in 1962. *Twelve Letters to a Small Town* published; won the Governor General's Award for the best volume of poetry published in 1962. *Wednesday's Child,* a satirical birthday card for "CBC Wednesday Night," performed on "CBC Wednesday Night" in December.

1963 *The Dance of Death at London, Ontario* published. *Names and Nicknames,* directed by John Hirsch and Robert Sherrin, performed nine times at the Manitoba Theatre Centre, Winnipeg, in November. *Twelve Letters to a Small Town* repeated on "CBC Wednesday Night" in September.

1965 *Let's Make a Carol: A Play with Music for Children* published. Wrote the libretto for *The Shivaree;* not yet performed or published. *The Boy with an R in His Hand* published. *The Sun and the Moon* produced in August by the Campus Players at London, Ontario. *Apple Butter* and *Little Red Riding Hood* produced at the Western Ontario Fair and at the Toronto Art Gallery. *The Killdeer* performed at the Glasgow Citizens' Theatre, Scotland, as part of the Commonwealth Arts Festival.

1966 *Listen to the Wind* performed by the Campus Players at London, Ontario, in August, and at the Robinson Memorial Theatre in Hamilton in October. John Andrew, his son, died, aged 11.

CHAPTER 1

Pluperfect Things

THE name of James Reaney first became known outside his home community of Stratford, Ontario, when as a student at the University of Toronto he began publishing short stories and poems in *Canadian Poetry Magazine, Canadian Forum, Contemporary Verse, Driftwind* (a little magazine published in Cleveland), *Here and Now, Northern Review,* and *The Undergrad.* It was the short stories which first drew attention to him, although his main reputation now is that of one of Canada's best poets who in recent years has turned to playwriting. The short stories are not numerous, only six having been published in the 'forties, and two later, in 1952, after he had moved to Winnipeg. They quickly gained a *succès de scandale* and a notoriety which their author half seriously suggests led to his Manitoban exile.

I *The Short Stories*

Reaney's short stories are skillfully constructed and with one or two exceptions deserve to be more widely known than they are, not only as things in themselves but as important early formulations of images and patterns still working almost two decades later in his mature writings. The fascination with the macabre, the concern with a split between a romantic world of art, music, and poetry and the dreary environment of a cultural backwater, and the depiction of a desperate tension between a febrile romantic sensitivity and a brutal repressive community—these are still the stuff of Reaney's art, although a good deal more has by now come into play.

The settings of all but one, "Mr. Whur: A Metamorphosis," are rural or small-town, and the central figure on whose feelings and thoughts the narrative is focused is, in five of the stories, a young woman whose secret emotions are in sharp conflict with the external circumstances of her life. For some reason all five young women have vaguely romantic sounding names ending in *a*—Emma, Roberta, Letitia, Sylvia and Irma. Beneath a tidy domestic surface of household or farm tasks the protagonist's intense need for rebellion is gradually realized and finally breaks out. In one story, "Dear Metronome," the rebellion is short-lived and Irma resumes her task of ministering to a very neurotic piano-teacher mother. The narrative style is consistently quiet and ironic, focusing on vivid details of a somewhat rococo imagery, as the stories build to climaxes of violence.

In "Clay Hole" the protagonist is Emma, something of an intellectual, unmarried but pregnant. She is trapped on her parents' farm, "feeding black Minorca hens and picking raspberries," and is overwhelmed by a future prospect of intolerable loneliness. In a setting closely based on an actual part of the Reaney farm, Emma quietly swims out into the deepest part of a pond where she sees the sun staring down "like a purple cabbage" as she drowns herself.

"The Box-Social," Reaney's most notorious composition, is the slow, deliberate account of a young woman, Sylvia, exercising a kind of pale white mental control as she prepares for a box-social. Throughout the narrative we observe her meticulous care in decorating, with gorgeous scarlet and gilt wallpaper, a "precious" shoe-box containing the lunch she will put up for auction. The teller builds carefully, providing several subtle clues but giving nothing away: "Little useless things," "twelve black hair-ribbons," "nightshade berries," "the children's desks were cowering in one corner." The central idea is Charles Addamsish, an arranging of the objects in a highly charged situation so that even the most grotesque fact is treated as a domestic detail subject to the housekeeper's tidying impulse, as in the Addams cartoon of a widow showing a visitor her deceased husband's effects all hanging in a long, neat row in the attic, at the end of which the eye comes to rest on the husband himself, also hanging. Reaney's piece has to do with wall-papering a very ugly experience into a pretty artifact where it can't hurt the protagonist-victim. The climax comes when the right man buys the box, and prepares to eat, but finds inside "the crabbed corpse of a still-born child wreathed in bloody newspaper." In retrospect, the story's most effective line is a snatch of conversation from the euchre game which at one point has interrupted the dancing; we have already been told twice how pale Sylvia is, so that when we read, "I pass, pale-face; joker," we see how the whole elaborate preparation is the by-passed, palefaced Sylvia's proof that she too is the grim joker, like her creator.

II The Red Heart *and Other Early Poems*

About two-thirds of Reaney's early poems, a number of them considerably revised, were gathered together in 1949 as *The Red Heart*. A collection of forty-two lyrics, this first book-length publication is an extraordinary achievement for a twenty-three-year-old poet and was immediately recognized as such by Canadian readers. Its five hundred copies sold out and have been Canadiana items for several years. Appearing towards the end of a decade in which Canadian poetry had on the whole been markedly social in its preoccupations, the intensely private quality of *The Red Heart* lyrics was startling and refreshing. The main focus of the book is on the figure of a youthful artist coming to poetic terms with a very particular environment. He imagines his life on earth as a continual retreat, but someday, he believes, he will be free to go back to the heaven he has lost.[1]

The world of *The Red Heart* is clearly imagined; like the early Edith Sitwell's Troy Park and the Brontës' Haworth Parsonage, it is palpable, immediate, confining. So far as it has an actual geographical location it is a farm near Stratford, Ontario, or, in one of the four cycles of poems which make up the book, the larger area of the Great Lakes system. Urban Ontario and the world beyond are dimly apprehended mysteries, perhaps to be explored in the future after escape from "this dull township / Where fashion, thought and wit / Never penetrate." Most of the poems are set in an old farmhouse or in the garden, fields, and lanes immediately outside. Such a setting might have been idyllically pastoral, with happy family life, easy work, games, singing, and the beauties of nature much in evidence, but *The Red Heart* makes only vestigial use of an unspoiled pastoral ideal.

The farmhouse is lonely and haunted, almost totally empty of human companionship, inhabited only by an unhappy child and pink and blue wallpaper, bannisters, staircases, mouse-holes, wardrobes, closets, and a clock which "with icetones . . . strikes." The title poem of the first cycle, "The Plum Tree," shows a day-dreaming child lolling "Among the trunks and featherticks / That fill the room where he was born" and im-agining the thoughts of his little sister as she died. Outside, in an old orchard, is a crooked plum tree from whose green heaven plump, ripe plums fall "as dead stars rush to a winter sea." In the near stillness there is a sense of quiet uneasiness, even dread, as "The plums . . . like blue pendulums . . . thrum the gold-wired winds of summer," hypnotically absorbing the reader into the world of the Red Heart. The themes—memory and dreaming in the imagination of a poetic child, falling from heaven, life in a haunted place, premature death—are not spelled out but make themselves known in the visual imagery and in the "thrumming" and "falling" musical effects of the strongly accen-tuated lines: "Only he hears their intermittent soft tattoo / Upon the dry, brown summer ground."

The primary impact of the farmhouse on the child's senses provides materials for rich fantasy. In "The Clouds" he sits out-side "as at play" watching the clouds weep and shake with thunderous laughter, but soon effects a mental withdrawal back into the confines of the house where "all the sky's become / A bedroom's wallpaper / Where vague white beasts / Jostle, slip and caper." The metamorphosis of natural phenomena into paper or cardboard is characteristic of several poems in *The Red Heart* and is one indication of a strong influence on the early Reaney of the early poems of Edith Sitwell.

"Gray Pillar," perhaps the most nearly perfect lyric in the book, connects the life of the solitary child moving about with "Cyclopean eye in the thisway / And the thatway of ban-nisters / And staircases" with the figure of an "excited skater" on a Christmas card. With "delicate foot" the figure on the paper twelve times strikes the "bell-like ice of clean water / Turned to glass," measuring, like the ice-toned clock in the house, the "life and love and childhood" of the poet and re-minding him of his "deathfulness." Like the scenes on Keats's Grecian urn, the one on the card depicts excitement, passion, and life permanently caught in the stasis of art ("Never never shall the ice melt") but also serves, paradoxically, to remind the poet that, like him, the farmhouse clock functions in the order of the actual. The diamond-footed skater's clarity of definition and his invulnerability to time and decay are set against another image on the card, a "yellow old willow" with "gold veins and arteries / Flowing, flowering into a wintry sky" whose "gray breast-bone" symbolizes the mortal labyrinth ending in death which is "The maze and passageways" of the child's life in the farmhouse. The little paper world momentarily defeats the inexorable clock.

The much anthologized piece, "The Katzenjammer Kids," derives from the same kind of fantasy. The "funny-paper" world of the Kids is highly abstract and stylized; its cardboard jungle and its brown-paper cannibals, and the ritual alternation of its life, between eating stolen fat pies made by the dear fat mother and being spanked by the blue Captain and the orange Inspector, are all symbolic of an imaginative reality at once more simple and more desirable than the actual world, for in this other world "the innocent childish heart" knows that the sun shines, despite cannibalistic feasts and spankings, and knows also that there is at least one loving parent.

Similarly, in "The Autobiography of a Marionette" the world inhabited by the central figure is made of cardboard, a box. Here, with a quill stolen from "a furious wren," an aging marionette urgently pens the story of his life as "a primary-coloured figure / In a fairy-tale." With feet shaped like those of a trout, he and his fellows live in an artificial order where strings control everything, from marriage to foxtrotting to death, since the "steely bands" which tie them are part of another more malignant order of things. In each of these poems—"Gray Pillar," "The Katzenjammer Kids," "The Autobiography of a Marionette" —and in others, active, vital figures move with gaiety in a world of pleasing artifice, but are always threatened by hostile forces which pull and yank, or quietly destroy.

The menaced paper world inside the fear-dominated house has its counterpart outside in the images of a natural order fundamentally destructive, despite its temporary achievements of fragile beauty. "The Sundogs" is the gleeful account of a barking conversation among the mythical animals of the Sun as they plot the rain, wind, and storm with which they'll drown crickets, set killdeer birds flying, pick apples ripe or not, and overturn hencoops, rabbit hutches, and privies (with people inside them). In the poet's handling of his subject, the ring around the moon, traditional herald of a coming storm, is an apparently innocent children's game about to go wild and plunge the whole rural landsape into chaos.

In a similar, myth-making style, "Suns and Planets" poses two questions, "Suns and planets of the sky / When will you be ripe and die?" and "Will a great wind sometime sweep / The dark branches where you weep . . . ?" The second question is elaborated by means of a metaphorical conceit in which the sky is an orchard of fruit trees, with red, yellow, and gold pears, apples, and plums set against dark branches, as mythical images of Venus, Mars, and Pluto respectively, waiting for the autumnal (Doomsday) destruction to come.

The recurrent Canadian nature myth of the indifference of the Canadian wilderness to human values gets ironic treatment in the first poem of "The Great Lakes Suite," the third cycle in The Red Heart. In a litany of self-approbation the cold and gray Lake Superior, which has "no superior," recounts how it chills the girls from Fort William so they cannot swim in it and sinks its drowned victim so deep that he is never found. Boasting, sadistic, and glittering in the northern light, the lake, whose "shores are made of iron" and "Lined with tough, wizened trees," is representative of a major mythical force in Reaney's writings, an almost Hardyesque abstraction of a power in nature surrounding human lives which exults in its capacity to torment and to claim victims.

In quieter vein, with a suggestion of melancholy, "Pink and White Hollyhocks" explores the theme of the fragility of any natural loveliness in a time-dominated world. Against a background of rural Ontario from June to autumn, in which farmers "shout gee and haw" in the fields and girls picking wild strawberries giggle in the ditches, the poet describes the growth, maturity, and death of a garden flower. Early summer is the time of noisy activity and rapid natural growth, mid-summer is more quiet and intense, and autumn is the silence of beauty consummated, followed by death. By this pattern of ascent ending in extinction the hollyhocks describe their brief existence; in June their green spires "spear" upwards; from July to September within the green towers they, like

> Ladies pre-raphaelite
> In their intense ascent
> Climb slowly to the topmost rooms
> With pink lamps and white lanterns.

And in autumn, when the garden is dying, they enter the highest chamber "Hung with citherns and lutes" and lie down with their lover, having blown out their pink lamps forever.

If, as I am suggesting, the archetypal myth taking new expression in the pages of *The Red Heart* is that of the threatened, precarious, or even vanished pastoral world, it is not surprising that flower images are rare. The old orchards, the dry brown summer ground, and the wintry gardens observed by the poet in whose body the Red Heart beats are not congenial to the mayflowers, dogtooth violets, and trilliums of the Ontario spring. There is a thicket of Jack-in-the-Pulpit plants, in the nightmare world of "A Fantasy and a Moral," late in the book, in which a demon lover deep in a moonlit forest claims the full-breasted body of a young woman, to impregnate it with a poisonous child and death. There are also violets, in one poem, completely divorced from a benign pastoral landscape and placed, satirically, in the midst of a dirty, sterile public beach. In "The Ivory Steeple" a despicable and wealthy esthete has among his luxuries "A Christmas rose on the window sill," while in "Antichrist as a Child" the flowers, and even the ugliest weeds of a mother's garden, avoid the fingers of her tormented, monstrous offspring.

The earth itself, whether associated with the farmhouse or with a more remote part of the world, is either fertile, but experiencing destruction, or moribund, and filled with grotesque shapes. Lightning flames in frightened trees, oats and barley are lodged in the ground, and wheat stooks are torn open by rain, wind, and storm. The ground in an orchard is mildewed and ragged with decaying fallen fruit and the autumn air is thick. Mountains are worn away by the labors of a mythical farmer, Weather, whose cattle have hooves of "limp water" working away throughout the ages. There are several winter gardens with stiff dead leaves "languageless with frost" in which the child-protagonist of the book vainly searches for happiness or encounters nightmarish beings.

One of the most persistent images in *The Red Heart*, associated with themes of falling and fatal determinism, is the gray grave into which all are trampled. In one poem, coffins are the eggs of "Queen Death" laid "in her cold nest," "the gravelly ancient breast / Of Earth." Then, altering the metaphor, the earth becomes a

> rotting head
> That like a criminal's face
> Severed and thrown from the block
> Tumbles round and round
> The pitying merciful Sun.

The theme of death and decay is given archetypal resonance when we are told that the first of Death's children was Abel, her nest-egg, and that she waits through the centuries for her children to hatch on "the branches of a dead tree."

No traditional pastoral streams of living water unify or give life to the landscapes of *The Red Heart*. In "The Upper Canadian," where the poet knows himself to be caught in a cultural backwater, the ineffectual wish is expressed that he had been born beside a river instead of a round pond. If this had been, he muses, he might have escaped his limited intellectual diet of closet Shakespeare, old Victorian novels, and "the dingy interwinding tunes / Of country rain and wind," and thus have overcome the "starved cricket" which is his mind. By the end of the poem, however, he has recognized that his cramped mind *is* the little pond where his "thoughts float round / As geese do round a pond / And never get out." Escape from the environs of Stratford still seems to be the answer but the glitter of darning-needle flies by the pond has its attraction, and so he waits for a miracle of deliverance that he knows will not come:

> I won't go away
> Unless it rains and rains
> Making the pond so large
> That it joins the river,
> But it never will.

Water as a symbol of bondage, this time to death, appears in
"Dark Lagoon," whose central metaphor is the identification
of a mother's womb with both a sunless lagoon and a grave.

Antithetically, in "The Two Kites," the "high, loud river of
the wind" flowing far above the earth is a place of life and
freedom remote from "the still, playbox air," the latter symbolizing the coffins down into which all eventually are pulled. When
water symbolism is a product of the child's delighted fantasy-
making, like the wallpaper and cardboard figures, it becomes
at once more stylized and more acceptable. A summer sky
transformed includes "white jumping mountains" whose down-
flowing streams are "long tall stilts of glass," clouds are composed "of swiftly sculptured rain," water beating on the roof of
the farmhouse makes "the noise of a thousand typewriters,"
and the "bell-like ice of clean water" has turned to glass in the
"Exquisite" world of a Christmas card scene.

Throughout the twenty-odd years in which he has been
writing poetry Reaney has never ceased to be fascinated with
birds and animals, many known to him from actual observation
on an Ontario farm but others deriving from more recondite
sources. In his later and more sophisticated writings this lore
makes its way into complex symbolic structures which do not
readily give up all their meaning. As one would expect, however, from what we have already seen of *The Red Heart* world,
its birds and animals are more simply used. At times the context is idealized and pastoral, at others it is one of nightmare
horror, and then again it is satirical or ironic.

In "The Plum Tree," with its narcotic rhythms and quiet
melancholy absorbing reader and day-dreaming child, a "happy"
cow apart from the child moos slowly and listlessly. The traditional pastoral animal, the sheep, does not appear in the external
world described by the poet but it does in the imaginings of
the Red Heart child, as "vague white beasts" jostling, slipping,
and capering in a wallpaper sky. There are "soft fat horses / That
draw Weather in his wagon." These have their demonic
opposite in "Dream within Dream" where the poet tells of
riding pillion with a demon on "a horse whose favourite
hay / Was human hair." Crickets, killdeers, hens, and rabbits
are part of a natural scene which, however threatened, is on

the whole benevolent. Geese are identified, semi-allegorically, with an Upper Canadian's intellectual undevelopment and with the silliness of U. S. visitors (Michigeese and Michiganders) who "In the days of yore" picked a fight with the poet and his friends by claiming to have "won the war." In a more artificial and perhaps therefore a more secure milieu, in "The Groats," we find wasps and bees ("furry as yellow and black / Fat sofas and chesterfields"), butterflies, and an Italian humming-bird. In the midst of the decisive black outlines of the funny-paper world of the Katzenjammer Kids, distant birds are drawn "like two eyebrows close together" and the dwarf imps them-selves have "porcupine locks."

As the imaginative terrain gives way to more bizarre fancies, in "Whither Do You Wander?" and "A Fantasy and a Moral," there is a sly fox threatening a forsaken child, and another one, angry with hunger, leaping at a would-be human victim as she flows past to an erotic rendezvous with a fiend. In the world of grotesques inhabited by the mammalian Miss Beatty of "A Fan-tasy and a Moral," sexual lust and death have their incono-graphic dimensions in the ancient snake, adder, and worms. And finally, explicitly allegorically, we have the bird known as "Queen Death" in "Coffins," the carrion-eating chough (in the poem by that name), "Whose name is Devouring Years" and, in the last poem of the book, the "bird of Paradise," fading, even though its brilliance has not been permitted to shine on many pages of *The Red Heart*.

Spring must come to the gardens and fields of this pastoral poetry, because plums do ripen and occasional flowers blossom, but there is little sense of nature in all her changing moods, especially her lighter ones. Autumn, dead gardens, lanes of leafless trees, leaves hanging "languageless with frost," and winter—these are the seasonal symbols which quickly succeed the marks of a more benevolent or vital natural order. There is at times a wild exuberance in human and natural life, to set in relief the dominant ennui and frustration, but more often than not the energies released are related to a theme of destruc-tion. This is a world abandoned by Adonis, kept alive by the beating of a child's red heart and by the emergence of a poetic consciousness.

The figure of the child varies considerably from poem to poem. At times it is "he," at times "she," occasionally it is even "we," but most often it is "I," which probably is meant to suggest a rough analogy but no easy equation with the poet's own early life. The age of the protagonist ranges, not chronologically, so far as the organization of the book is concerned, from the unborn state to young adulthood. But youth has a way of aging quickly in *The Red Heart;* as soon as there is even a rudimentary consciousness, the child is aware of time and death. In "Dark Lagoon" an infant has just come from the fetal world where the mother's heart was the distant tick-tocking of the chisel that would one day carve his name on a monument. The baby is still very young, but the poet describing him is rather old-mannish, prematurely disillusioned with the world of human experience. He has lived long enough to hear

> The cry of "Eenie, meenie, minie, moe,"
> By which children choose a loser in a game,
> And by which Fate seems to choose
> Which children shall be which:
> One-eyed, wilful, hare-lipped, lame,
> Poor, orphans, idiots, or rich.

Fate has chosen several ways of making children losers. The figures of orphans recur several times and two poems are given over entirely to their perspective. In "The English Orphan's Monologue" an angry, resentful hired girl, transplanted across the Atlantic waves from a London slum, feels herself enslaved on the farm where she lives and works. With a sadistic glee worthy of one of Browning's obsessed characters, she sits by the stove in the evenings plotting her revenge.

Generically the poem is a dramatic monologue, an anatomy of hatred in four stanzas. In each metaphorical conceit used by the speaker to reveal her situation she is a physical object with a specific utilitarian function exploited by her captors: they starch her arms and legs as if she were a dress, they put bits, saddles, and whiffletrees on her, and they muzzle her like a dog, but her wild, rebellious heart retains a kind of freedom. In stanzas two and three a double analogy between her heart and the fire and between her body and the kitchen stove is intricately developed and allowed to take into itself other incongruously appropriate ones: her flaming heart is like the lively yellow honey of Samson's lion, "a yellow hand in Hell / Ringing an evil crackling bell," "The hands of a demon gentleman" with orange and yellow nails, and so on. By stanza four simile gives way to complete identity: "I am the stove in which my heart hides." The multiplication of images one after the other vividly conveys the wild amoral force of hatred built up when love has been denied too long; the girl's rage has become "A greedy cruel hand that no dyke / Of morality can stop" and destruction must follow. Her revenge will be in two parts: she will "prune" the "Mr." for whom she works of his "nicest choicest limb" and she will get pregnant by the eldest son Harry, and so have them both thrown out.

In "The Orphanage" the plain white faces of children in yellow dresses peer through gray windows, as their owners think about the lust of the "young men who play hockey in winter" and "crawl over ghastly women" in the summer. They think also about their connection with a whore called "Miss Mumblecrust," who has scimitar earrings and a mouth watering for "the hard caramel bellies" of young men: "We are the answers / To those equations / In ditches and round-shouldered cars." But from such unions springs life and therefore the possibility of all the dirty tricks an adult world can play on a child. The sense of deep offense at the sexuality of men and women, a theme which runs through much of the book, stems from the wretchedness of the child's experience, all of which of course would have been impossible had he never been born.

On the whole the adult world comes off very badly in *The Red Heart*. When the child is not forlorn in his isolation, he is "stepmotherishly haunted" or threatened by some other parental figure of oppression and cruelty; in one poem he encounters a sly fox in his den, "as charming and good-mannered / As the President of France, / But his kitchen-floor he's scrubbing / With a tub of blood." A school teacher is tall, cold, and authoritarian. God is just as bad, known only to the small boy as the one who will send a bear to eat him up if he swears. In "The Two Kites" the malevolent power is simply "Someone." Lusting, blind, malevolent, sadistic, or cold and impersonal, whichever the individual adult is, he represents the dashing of childish impulses and desires by a harsh superego order of things. In a few poems the adults are only fools, the victims of their own stupidity.

There are, however, a few exceptional adults who are neither sadists nor fools. The "dear fat mother" of the Katzenjammers keeps only "fairly good guard" over the fat pies she bakes. We have already noticed the pre-Raphaelite hollyhock ladies in their love quest. In "A Miscellany," characterized by epigrammatic brevity and wit, Jane Austen's ironic capacities for exposing intellectual retardation and false moral values are turned on a girl whom the protagonist of "The Upper Canadian" must have seen many times in his dull township:

> You bore me, said a young ninny,
> With a very lipstick-clogged whinny,
> To Jane Austen.
> I rather think, said the author of Emma,
> That I would,
> And that it is, my dear, your dilemma!

The Red Heart describes, as its main emotional dialectic, a mixture of nostalgia and contempt in relation to the two worlds experienced by the poetic child, nostalgia when the frustrated desire has been moving in the direction of a fantastic, superior reality, contempt when a poem is focused on the adult world's blindness and malevolence. One might expect that a child's life so seriously and continuously threatened would result in the writing of elegy, in laments for a lost happiness or for a potential happiness never enjoyed. But Reaney, however "romantic" in his attraction to a world of marvels and idealized forms created by the human imagination, is not prone to extensive use of elegiac and idyllic themes. Already, for whatever literary and personal reasons, there had developed by the time of his first volume of lyrics considerable ironic detachment, to set beside the finely wrought texture and harmony of mood achieved in poems like "Gray Pillar" and "The Plum Tree" and to contrast with the lyric sense of shock and longing following a premature loss of innocence. Irony, when it is sustained, is the death of elegy, inasmuch as the elegiac attitude requires a strong and fairly explicit belief in ideals, a faith either that something better once existed or, at the very least, could have. Still, one has only to consider contemporary ironic fictions to recognize how a submerged romanticism gives point and resonance to the dinginess of the realities described in ironic myth. Beckett's *Endgame,* for example, with its use (in the English-language version prepared by the author) of Shakespeare's line "Our revels now are ended," seems unmistakably to point up the way the "anti-romance" nature of the play involves an exploitation of romance connotations to give an undertow of meaning.

The reviews and gossip surrounding the publication of *The Red Heart* made much of its romantic, even sentimental account of tormented childhood on an Ontario farm and also of its nightmarish fantasies, with the result that a myth of Reaney as a kind of pathetic *enfant terrible* of Canadian literature is still around. This, I suggest, ignores the ironic, objective qualities present in the poet's handling of his images and themes.

Part of the trouble, one suspects, is simply a failure by some to recognize that lyric poetry is based on an associative rhetorical process closely involved in the unconscious of the poet, where sound-links, ambiguous verbal connections, illogical associations, and dreamlike sequences are all working to produce a recognizably lyrical fusion of sound and sense which has a comprehensible form but is not necessarily much connected with the external facts of the poet's life. On the pages of *The Red Heart* one finds, on the one hand, private utterances precisely expressed, in unpredictable and irregular stanzaic patterns, and, on the other, witty or satirical pieces whose impulse is not towards a unified pattern of feeling but towards laughter and detachment.

Only ten of the twenty-three poems which make up "The Plum Tree" and "The School Globe" groupings—that is, the lyrical core of *The Red Heart*—are written in the first person singular and only one (possibly two) of the nineteen remaining pieces is. A large proportion focus the reader's attention on a third person or object. Several are dialogues rather than lyrics; and dialogue objectifies, sets the artist at a distance, or out of the matter altogether. Even in the first-person lyrics there is almost no self-pity; the situation described may be pathetic to the reader but the victim has more interesting devices than lamenting for expressing himself.

[30]

The most elaborate compensation the Red Heart has for the deprivation of human love is a rich life of fantasy, some of it liberating but some of it simply an extension of horror already realized. Out of the identification, in "The Clouds," of a summer afternoon sky with a bedroom's wallpaper comes a fanciful extravaganza on the childhood game of "counting sheep." Among the clouds are "hundreds of pairs / Of pink sofas and chairs," "great pink lutes," "soft pink boots," "Pink swollen violins," "Fat naked gentlemen whose sins / Have made them fat," and "at least a vat / Of Swans and gramophones." But the reverie on these wallpapered works of "the Marchioness of Madness" comes to an end with the disappointing thought, "They were only clouds." The longing for the world of pure metaphor remains, however, the desire that the fantasies be true: "What are the clouds that sail by so slow . . . / If not that fancied wallpaper . . . ?"

This is all harmless enough, but there are other poems filled with sinister imaginings. In "Dream within Dream," nightmare images fit "into each other / Like the dungeons and cells / Of a great dark jail," depicting the poet's sense of his life as one of predetermined dark horror. Each violent act he commits in the nightmare is preceded by the feeling that he has wakened just before he strikes out—to kill a man, to push a woman over a cliff, to choke "a vivacious gentleman," and finally to stab a girl "on an ottoman." Through the non-logic of dream and metaphor there is a progressive development of the idea that what at first seems to be separate and distinct is not really so but simply one in a series of images for the same emotional reality, an intense hatred directed towards parents, self, and life as such:

> Each time the face of the man became
> More like my father's face;
> And that of the woman, of course,
> Began to seem like my mother's,
> As if I could have slain my parents
> For that foul deed that struck
> Me out of chaos, out of nothing.

Exhausted and struggling to get free of the dream horror, he prays to Heaven "With its thousand white stars" somehow to stop his maddened mind. The violence of the nightmare and the

depth of the "bad despair" which caused it leave him plunged
in lassitude and uncaring, to dream one last time, of himself as
a lifeless "sack of blood and bones" or "pillar of dust."

The destructive fantasy, as a means of hitting back, is a theme
which recurs throughout the book. It may be treated playfully,
as in "The Sundogs"; these animals, who stand ready to obey
the Sun's "most auburn wish / For Rain, Wind and Storm,"
take puppyish delight in reducing a scene of rural quiet to wild
anarchy. In "Suns and Planets" the artist looks for the "thick
autumn time" when a great wind will pluck down the heavenly
bodies. One of the children in *The Red Heart* wonders why he
traces the letter *A* on a windowsill, because *his* name contains
no *A;* he wonders why his mother looks at him so sadly, why
his father stares, and why even nature draws back at his touch.
When his feet become hooves and make his shoes pinch, he does
not let on, lest he be shot for a monster. His dreams have to
do with eclipses of the sun, sunsets, and the turning upside down
of the works of human civilization. Not until later does he learn
that he is Antichrist.

To strike back is one possibility. To become an inanimate object, for instance a top on a string, is another; then, after crazy
spinning periods, one can have long intervals of peaceful rest.
One can also withdraw into the past, regress, refuse to go on;
this theme is especially persistent in Reaney's writings and is
best illustrated in *The Red Heart* by the retrospective poem
"The School Globe." Here we have the timeless structure of
elegy skillfully adapted to a particular human being and situation; the elegist, in this case a prematurely disillusioned adolescent boy, stands alone in a deserted place musing on the past
("Sometime in the summertime / All alone in an empty school-
room"). As he summons up the remembrance of things past,
he longs for the restoration of his happy childhood times. A
"faded old globe" held in his hands brings memories of lessons,
games, tops, pets, and, especially, of the house where he was
little, with its rooms where he was as old as he was high. These
things he once loved were more than perfect; in a sense they
were always "past," for the Red Heart born an exile from the
paradise of childhood. Only because of a nostalgia fostered by
time and an intense desire never fulfilled have "the fair fields

and lands" of his childhood ever been created: "This school globe is a parcel of my past, / A basket of pluperfect things." Still, he would gladly go back:

> if someone in authority
> Were here, I'd say
> Give me this old world back
> Whose husk I clasp
> And I'll give you in exchange
> The great sad real one
> That's filled
> Not with a child's remembered and pleasant skies
> But with blood, pus, horror, death, stepmothers, and lies.

Through all his wanderings and experiences the bearer of the Red Heart is engaged in a quest initiated by one overriding, if futile, wish:

> wherever I go,
> Wherever I wander
> I never find
> What I should like to find;
> For example, a mother and father
> Who loved me dearly
> And loved each other so,
> And brothers and sisters with whom,
> In the summer, I'd play hide-and-go-seek
> And in the winter, in the snow,
> Fox-and-goose week after week.
> Instead I must forever run
> Down lanes of leafless trees
> Beneath a Chinese-faced sun;
> Must forsaken and forlorn go
> Unwanted and stepmotherishly haunted
> Beneath the moon as white as snow.

Failing in the search for a happy family, the Red Heart turns away from this world altogether and for a time becomes mistress of a golden lover, the Sun. In "Dark Lagoon" a child still in the prenatal state is aware of a double paradox, that the mother's heart heard in the distance is the life-giving Sun but is also a clock "with little clicking mouthfuls" devouring the time of the child's life; it is also a chisel in the hand of a monument-maker, carving the child's epitaph.

In a few poems the large betrayal of conception, birth, and life is for a time obliterated. "The Heart and the Sun," which has more of a narrative line than most of *The Red Heart* poems, involves the giving and accepting of an invitation to love. The life of the lovers passes and the death of one of them ends the union. The impulse of the poem is markedly mythopeic, the language richly suggestive. The Heart is a containing metaphor for the earthly recipient of life and love and the Sun is the eternal, masculine bestower of a life capable of entering time. The longing of the beating, gasping Heart in this poem is also the fundamental emotion in the romantic myth described throughout the book; the desire for union with the kingdom of the Sun (expressed also in "The Plum Tree," "The Sundogs," and "Suns and Planets") is one variant of a romantic aspiration towards a fulfilling, harmonious vision of beauty and power, as the means of transcending the confinement and death of a purely earthly existence.

Like many romantic poems, however, "The Heart and the Sun" is a description of a failure to sustain the miraculous marriage of earth and heaven precariously called into being. The enemy is time. When the Heart is "ripely heavy with age," winter wind and cold pluck down the red leaf and the gold prisoner falls into lamentation over his dead red mistress whose sweet rooms now swarm with decay. In the title poem of the book, which follows immediately, the question is asked, "Who shall pick the sun / From the tree of Eternity?" and the answer comes back, "It seems that no one can." The result of this negation is, according to the story of the Red Heart, destruction for all things of radiance and beauty in the mutable world.

Each reaction of the child to the world of experience leads to a dead end, to the gray grave where all shall be trampled. Throughout it all runs the horror of the dark sensuality which brings the baby into the world. It is, then, a mark of the ambiguity of this early volume, that the one remaining possibility, one which emerges fitfully throughout and more insistently towards the end, is the love of man and woman. At times its treatment is ironic and closely associated with themes of death. In "A Fantasy and a Moral" the young woman with ballooning

breasts who is wafted into a Keatsian lunar forest to enjoy a
ghostly love is deluded and doomed:

> So love, though measured breath by breath,
> May seem like walking in a summer dream,
> Visiting nowhere but pleasant places;
> So love does often lead a filthy way to Death.

A more idyllic view of love appears in the poem "To My
Love," where we see opening up one of the themes which, later,
in *A Suit of Nettles* and the plays, are set against those childhood attitudes we have been considering. Even in this poem,
though, the movement towards physical union with another
adult is tentative, the imagery is highly abstract, and the love
suggested is obviously (because of the traditional associating of
it with a death-urge) no more than the first "fantastic" experience of eros:

> Though I've devoured all substance
> In twenty-one years,
> I shall not, must not die
> Until, my Love,
> Like a fantastic white glove
> You my hand
> (Each finger for a special sense)
> Tries on
> Then dig my grave
> For I am ripe
> For senseless, languageless lifelessness.

The Red Heart terminates in an epitaphial poem with the
mythological title "The Bird of Paradise." Here we have the
conclusion of the theme of the threatened pastoral. The paradisal bird as it fades into nothingness is associated with the
Ace of Spades turning gray, with a "once loud bell" cracking,
and with the fires of Hell being extinguished. Any possible romantic notion that either the poet or his book is immortal is
carefully expunged:

> So my tongue like the wick
> Of a lamp shall someday fail
> Of any glinting words and pale
> Shall falter with a sigh and pout
> That all Fire, all Hell, all Poetry is out.

The Red Heart contains several finely executed lyrics and it
has an overall shape for its romantic and ironic accounts of the
experiences of the Red Heart. There is in the book an unmistakable drive and energy, a love of poetic inventiveness and
experiment, and a willingness to strike out new and palpable
images or unusual rhythms. If the performance is irregular at
times, and it is (there are a few of the poems, not many, which
might better have been omitted or placed differently), this is
because Reaney in 1949 had not yet achieved the close synthesis of emotion and intellect which is one of the really extraordinary things about his more recent writings.

The Red Heart, for all its ironic wit and poignant beauties, is
probably best understood as a book of beginnings, of attempts
to handle large matters, both poetic and existential. As one
rereads it, even setting aside a knowledge of the later works,
there is a notable sense of one literary experience or imaginative
attempt inducing another, of myths, legends, nursery rhymes,
children's games, rural sights, sounds, and smells, and rhythmical
structures all fitting gradually into a larger pattern. A good
deal has rightly been made, in reviews and commentaries, of
the role of the actual geographical locale of Stratford, Ontario,
in these poetic skirmishes. This, to my mind, is the least of the
matter, for the actual environment and the boy called James
Reaney in it are at most the pseudo-contents of *The Red Heart*.
What is seeking expression here is something that Reaney himself would now readily recognize, that peculiar variant of pastoral described in the preceding pages, something at once less
ephemeral than an individual place, personality, and experience,
and a basis on which imaginative growth is possible. Still, it is
easy to understand how the intensely personal quality of the
poems and the distinctively macabre vision of reality in the
volume have led some readers to indulge in biographical speculation, rather than staying with the more critically rewarding
work of examining the particular literary transfiguration of the
Stratford environs achieved by a precocious and compelling new
poetic voice.

One gathers from reviews and other comments on some of
Reaney's later works that there are readers who would have
preferred him to go on inhabiting the world of the Red Heart,

with its relative lack of literary sophistication and its essentially discontinuous lyric art. This is a little like wishing Yeats had stayed with Innisfree. In a sense, though, these readers can have half of their wish fulfilled, in any of three ways. The highly personal and lyric qualities of the early collection are present, sporadically or more pervasively, in most of what has followed. Secondly, several important lyrics have been published separately during the 'fifties and 'sixties while others have been written but are still waiting for their author to decide on an overall organization for them. To date he has considered two possibilities: a collection of the scattered compositions into a forty-eight piece grouping, based on the structure of the Well-Tempered Clavier of Bach; or, with the help of an artist, an emblem book. The third continuation of his early lyricism and miniaturist scale of writing is the widely praised, even widely loved, *Twelve Letters to a Small Town.*

III   Twelve Letters to a Small Town

The *Letters*, published in 1962, were long in the making. They are, as a glance at the Bibliography at the end of this book will show, only one of many items produced in the thirteen years after *The Red Heart*, including the complex long poem *A Suit of Nettles* and several of the plays. The "First Letter," addressed, in the epistolary style of the whole, to the Avon River above Stratford, Canada, was published in *Canadian Forum* in February, 1951. The lyric entitled "The Storm," on page 20 of the book, was published, in a version as yet unadapted for the Stratford milieu of the *Letters*, in the University of Toronto undergraduate daily, *The Varsity*, in January, 1960.

The *Letters* are a suite of lyrics, prose poems, dialogues, and verbal games in the form of a libretto or "little book" set to music for a chamber orchestra (flute, piccolo, oboe, guitar, piano, and harmonium) by John Beckwith. They were made available to the public first as a radio program on the CBC's "Wednesday Night" series in July, 1961. The production was by John Reeves, himself a poet and playwright as well as a producer. The radio version was repeated once, in September, 1963, after the publication of the book. The printed text is, with minor variations, what the radio listeners heard.

One view of *Twelve Letters to a Small Town* is that it represents a return on Reaney's part to his true genius as a lyric poet, after a corrupting or misguided sojourn in the wilderness of academe with its literary sophistication, and also after a few wrongheaded attempts to work as a playwright, something for which he clearly did not have what it takes. Both parts of this view are, in my opinion, wrong: Reaney's lyric powers are not exclusive of others, nor are they in danger of dying out, and his recent writing for the theater is certainly more richly inventive than anything else in Canada at present. Still, there is a palpable connection between the *Letters* and *The Red Heart* in the fact that the imagery of pluperfect things is central in each and that of irony and satire more incidental. In the more pronouncedly satirical writings—*A Suit of Nettles,* "A Message to Winnipeg," *The Dance of Death at London, Ontario,* and *One-man Masque*— the pattern has the opposite emphasis, as the myth changes to one of realistic depiction, however exaggerated, of an actual historical society, and as pastoral themes are used to point up the absurdity and grotesqueness of the society in question.

An anonymous reviewer in one of the Quebec newspapers expressed this reaction to the way Reaney, in the *Letters,* has fashioned from droll, humorous materials serious poetry: "J'aime cette poésie allègre, souriante, tendrement enfantine, sans être infantile." This could not have been said of *The Red Heart,* despite the important similarities of the two books, for *The Red Heart* in its main contours is not a happy, smiling book.

The basic connection between these two distinct versions of pastoral, one of a threatened and insecure world, the other of a world at once harmonious and intact, lies in the continuation of the childlike vision deriving from the poet's intensely felt relation to the Stratford environment. The fundamental difference is that the *Letters* are the work of a mature man whose poetic vision has clarified and whose craftsmanship has improved, so that he exhibits a highly controlled and conscious lyricism rather than the brilliant yet threatened youthful sensibility of *The Red Heart.* There is not the high degree of romantic tension, of destructive versus benign influences, nor is there the sharp polarization of emotions characteristic of much of Reaney's writings, early and late. There is gentle irony, even satire (the irony and satire in *The Red Heart* are angrier, more abrasive, sometimes bitter) but not enough to undercut or dispel the prevailing easy, unforced romanticism. The *Letters* are written by someone who has gone away from his birthplace and now sees it in perspective, as the physical and spiritual environment which helped shape him as poet. As we shall observe later, this creating of a poetic fiction out of the artist's own environment and experiences, this concern to show the creation of an esthetic sensibility in a particular kind of setting, is basic to Reaney's own peculiar brand of romantic art, and it is a process which he has continued in almost everything he has written. But *Twelve Letters to a Small Town* is a quite different handling of the subject from that found in all the other works except one, the opera *Night-blooming Cereus*. Only in these two compositions does the vision of an unspoiled pastoral ideal emerge as almost free from the threatening influences which surround the desires of the Red Heart, or of the boy-artist figure in the later works.

The point of cynosure for the Red Heart's imagination is the farmhouse, however far beyond its confines his fancies take him. The center of attraction for the adolescent boy in the *Letters* is the small town of Stratford, remembered from the late 'thirties and early 'forties. He is presented as very much a farm boy, drinking in the sights and sounds of the town. The farmhouse has become the secure center from which, by bicycle or red-wheeled buggy, he makes his way along the gravel road and the highway into town. The farm is no longer associated with the pathos of the Red Heart child's futile search, nor with his wild, destructive fantasies. Significantly, it is conceived in terms of a happy marriage in whose context children play and farm work is done. Even an element of violence is easily contained:

> Out here barn is wedded to house,
>   House is married to barn,
>   Gray board and pink brick.
>   The cowyard lies between
> Where in winter on brown thin ice
>   Red capped children skate.
> There is wallpaper in the house
>   And in the barn
> They are sawing the horns off a bull.

The age of the Red Heart ranges all the way from the prenatal period to the threshold of manhood. In keeping with the more closely unified character of the *Letters* the age span is precisely delimited, to that time "Halfway between childhood & manhood" when the boy has begun to dream of "the two-backed beast" (the fantasy gets its image from literature not life) and to feel "The accumulating sexual yeast." Here we do not have the unhappy ravaging "teenager" of contemporary North American and English popular cinematic conventions but rather a very live, imaginative boy, superbly gifted with a capacity to see mystery and wonder in the simplest, most familiar things. As readers of the *Letters,* we are involved with two poets, the one James Reaney at the age of thirty-five or thirty-six, when the book took final shape, the other his creation or persona, the imaginative adolescent student through whom we are invited to undergo the particular experiences involved in this recreation of an actual place.

The "First Letter" is a lyric addressed "To the Avon River Above Stratford, Canada." It begins with a question, "What did the Indians call you?" and goes on to explore the nature of the river in terms of its impact on the senses of the poet, but the poem does not answer the question. The central, organizing metaphor lies in the close identification of poet and river. The river does "not flow / with English accents" and it "did not taste English" to him when as a boy he drank it with his cupped hands. It was the first river he ever crossed and is therefore his "law" for all others; the Red and the Thames, which flow through the two other centers in which Reaney has lived, "Are never so sweet. . . ." The sentence of this river's voice "With a soprano / Continuous cry" will always flow through his heart. As the poet rejects the English name and character of the river (Avon, bards) and defines it instead in terms of Canadian images ("the sad wild fowl" in Audubon prints, reeds, cresses, sedges, crayfishes, muskrats, and farmers' geese), it merges in an unobstrusively mythopeic way as a spirit of Ontario nature and, at the same time, as the symbolic source of the poet's own vocation. The literary prototype for this lyric, perhaps even the "source," appears to be the description of the English Thames in "Cooper's Hill" by the seventeenth-century poet Sir John Denham.

[40]

Through vividly realized images, connoting the intensity and sweetness of first experience, and in a mood of nostalgia completely free of any cloying emotionalism, the poem builds to its lyric climax in the poet's telling the river one of his earliest wishes, "To flow like you." With this use of the archetypal image of flowing water as the source of poetry there is another image, equally familiar, in the poet's promise to the river that through the craft of poetry he will immortalize it: "The rain and the snow of my mind / Shall supply the spring of that river / Forever."

A reference to the "dear bad poets / Who wrote / Early in Canada / And never were of note" expands the theme but does not detract from the highly personal nature of the lyric. Reaney writes with a sense of coming late enough in a native Canadian poetic tradition for that tradition to have matured sufficiently for good poetry to emerge and be recognized. In this faith (the right word) and with this book, commissioned by the publicly-owned CBC, we can see one of the exciting facts of contemporary Canada which enabled the writers of the 945-page *Literary History of Canada* to organize their story of Canadian literature from the earliest times to the present under the four headings "New Found Lands," "The Transplanting of Traditions," "The Emergence of a Tradition," and "The Realization of a Tradition."[2] Reaney's poetry is always highly individual, as it clearly is in this lyric, but he also has a deep sense of being one, and only one, relatively late representative of a Canadian tradition of poetry which becomes less inglorious as it matures. *Twelve Letters to a Small Town* is, among other things, a celebration of this cultural and biographical fact.

The "Second Letter" recalls the miniaturist art of the early short story "Mr. Whur: A Metamorphosis," in which an artist is absorbed out of the actual world into his tiny, intricate world of artifacts. Here we have a poem in the form of a dialogue between A and B, with A giving instructions on how to make a model of Stratford and B doing what he is told, as well as making some suggestions of his own. Through a process of playful imagining, Stratford becomes an arrangement of sticks, leaves, blue glass bubbles, and local farm fruit and vegetables inhabited by lady and gentleman bugs. In this reduction of a town to very simple elements there is a certain accuracy of observation involved which has little to do with naturalistic realism in description. When we are told that ripe gooseberries are being used for red houses and white raspberries for yellow brick houses, and that these are interspersed with white and red currants and cherries, a moment's recollection will remind us that a ripe gooseberry, with its lighter veined markings, is rather like a house with different sections and that it is a quite different kind of house from a larger, yellow raspberry one, with its more numerous small sections. Similarly, the Edward Lear absurdity of having apples for the business places on Main Street contains a grain of common sense, if one is willing to allow that there is some kind of connection between the traditional enticement symbolism of apples and the basic principles of selling.

The "Third Letter" continues the miniaturist style in its artistic simplification of a complex festival of sights and sounds—the annual Orangemen's parade on the Twelfth of July—first to its four main images and then to one all-inclusive one. To begin, we have the following: the local exemplar of King William, a white horse, Queen Mary, and an orange lily in the hand of each "regal" figure. By the end, in a sort of *reductio ad absurdum* artifice, the barely concealed eroticism of the man and woman "riding . . . With a white horse / In their groin" is neatly pointed up by the drawing provided by the poet; the prancing white charger, with flowing mane and tail, and with encircled asterisk or bicycle-wheel feet, and a crown on his head, has become the whole unified royal image.

In the "Fourth Letter," sub-titled "Voices and Prepositions," we are invited to follow the eye of the poet as it moves and takes in the buildings, structures, and objects of the town. In the five stanzas, each with its italicized epigraph involving an impressionistic image ("The roof of a small brewery by moonlight"), there are thirty-six localizing prepositions which in their aggregate, give the Letter its auditory and visual shape and at the same time allow an apparent randomness in the selection of images: "Up here is the Water Tower, down there's the Sewage Farm"; "on the back of his neck"; "with a branch of lilac in her hand"; "up . . . across, up . . . along . . . into, Across . . . on, Through . . . with," and so forth.

The images, in the main, depict sights familiar to Stratfordians even today in the 'sixties. The more bizarre details are part of

[42]

an overall harmony different from the antithetical structures of *The Red Heart*. Along with the Stone Bridge, the Dam, the Theatre, and the eggs and gladiolis in the market, we have an old Negro with a lump on the back of his neck and a girl with no hair, playing by the dam. It is a measure of the overall serenity and joy of the *Letters* that these latter, slightly grue-some images are not given prominence. The Sunday factory in the waste outskirts is "Like a monastery: lonely, empty, austere," not noisy and jangling with workers and machines. In addi-tion to the many points in space visited by the poet's eye there are three in time—"Sitting forever in the silent Saturday summer sun," a Sunday in June, and the noisy, happy Christmas season— which manage to suggest a timelessness and a ritualistic sense of simple, uncomplicated actions caught forever in their most characteristic gestures. Reaney's Stratford has been absorbed into the quiet stasis of one kind of pastoral art, into which no uneasy emotion or fear intrudes to recall that the lilac will wither or that the hundred gold-paper Christmas-tree angels will disappear.

The next two Letters abandon the panoramic view of the fourth and center attention on particular buildings and, more pre-cisely, on the mental processes of the people inside them. The "Fifth Letter" has to do with intellectual awakening, the sixth with mental torpor of the kind deplored but succumbed to in "The Upper Canadian." In the fifth, the Stratford High School is set in a very wide, archetypal context; it is "the palace of Merlin and Cheiron / Where the governors and governesses teach / The young Achilles and young Arthurs of the town." Most of the images are of things so ordinary they would go unnoticed unless claimed by an imaginative eye, but the mythi-cal frame of reference and the poet's extraordinary skill in vest-ing simple things with large conceptual significance lift the piece far above the level of pedestrian description. The two funda-mental languages whose mystery makes one human, words and numbers, are indicated in a Pauline image, completely adapted and at home in the Stratford High School: "In the dusty looking glass of grammar, / Number, the young see the shape of their brain." Empirical sensations provided by the stuffed bird, the coat hooks, and the snow-dripping windows instruct the lively mind of the boy-poet at least as much as the formal curriculum does. "The radiators teach the rule of monotony / Cheep cheep cheeping in the winter classroom."

It is in the "High, dark, narrow" cloakroom, however, that an image containing the whole mystery of being appears to the boy, and takes permanent possession of part of his mind:

> And I, lingering rearranging my books
> See sweeping face peer in of janitor
>   Alone in the winter twilight
>   The old janitor! An image to ponder over.

This figure of an aged Cheiron-like wise man, "In some way so centre and core," to whom the young look for help in coming of age, is one pondered by Reaney in most of his dramatic writings. Here the magisterial figure poses "a curious question" and elicits from the poet's imagination a figure of creativity released, of beautiful forms set free:

> the moon each month unlocks
> upon the wave
> A white bird.

The same boy, now described as an "awkward fool," appears again in the "Sixth Letter," as the boarder living with aging aunts in "A House on King William Street" where, like the wallpaper, the life endlessly repeats itself and no sense of novelty or beginnings disrupts the ongoing mindlessness. The names of the aunts—Aunt Henny and Aunt Penny, Aunt Lurkey and Aunt Turkey—sets the right beast-fable note for a satire on the limited mental horizons of small town people, stuck like wallpaper flowers to their particular spots, never changing their likenesses through the years but most of them losing their original blaze. The snatches of dialogue show Aunt Henny clucking about a shocking book she has just read. It is one of Reaney's favorites, H. Ryder Haggard's *She*, a story about an immortal woman called Ayesha who is inspired by an undying love and who lives deep in a mountain in the interior of East Africa; here she bathes in the flames of the Place of Life while she waits through the centuries for the arrival of her nineteenth-century reincarnated lover, the young Englishman Leo Vincey. Aunt Henny's experience of sensational fiction is clearly in sharp contrast to the outer dullness of her routine existence.

The "Seventh Letter" is in two closely related parts, one in the form of prose recollections of nineteenth-century life in Stratford, the other a poetic soliloquy by one of the figures from the past, an aged harridan called Granny Crack. The prose is impressionistic, non-assertive, a series of pictures from the past called up in the poet's mind by his reading of the tea-colored files of the town's newspapers in the archives of the Public Library. The details selected are of two sorts, those indicating the large changes between the past and the present and those found exciting enough by the inhabitants of the past to be included in the newspaper. Reaney shows his insight into the sharply individualized and stratified quality of life in the Victorian period of Canadian social history: "In the past people showed what they thought of themselves much more openly than they do now." He singles out a doctor's wife "of high degree" walking down Wellington Street with her nose literally in the air and an Indian woman who pulls flax and drinks vinegar. The unusual events which captured the interest of the writers of the papers include accounts of the crimes tried at the fall Assizes (the tavern stabbing of a Swiss traveller), bears running away with little boys, Indians stealing clothing while the owner was swimming, two boys called David and Jonathan drowning in the river, and the coming of the Crimean War.

Most of this Letter works in visual imagery, but there is also a successful recapturing of the rhythms and the sounds of Stratford throughout her one century of life. The winters were long we are told, and so uneventful that all that happened was snow. "Then in the spring the heart begins to beat more quickly again and there are actually more words in the paper." The poet hears carriage wheels, "grinding, singing, creaking, whirling in a fountain of sound at the place where the four branches meet" (the street branches from "Second Letter").

When the description moves away from the documentary style into something more metaphorical, the theme emerges; a flower or seed pod of all the words spoken at the crossroads of the town bursts open to reveal figures from the deep past which the poet did not have to read about because he heard of them from the voices of older people, or saw them once with his own eyes. Ancestral voices haunt us and we live, the author seems to be saying, especially the voice of Granny Crack, which tells of a hard life of "Trading and begging and fighting" as she, the repository of "the curious wisdom of brambles / And weeds, of ruts, of stumps and of things despised," wandered the country roads. This "incredible crone" is, in Reaney's Canadian mythology, a spirit of the rural Ontario countryside, elemental in her association with the sun and moon but intimately involved with the ongoing life of the "berry picking kids" who run in fear from her; her veins are their paths and roads and she is the darling of their god.

As the embodiment of a female principle in the countryside, Granny Crack has her masculine counterpart in "The old man of the town," the Winter Janitor, the two of them "Revolving back to back" in the poet's mind and looking down on his town. Reaney is perhaps saying here that a simple recalling of the economic and social facts of our historical past will not take us far on the mental voyage to imaginative maturity. What is needed is a coming to terms with the essence of the particular physical environment which has made us what we are, a recognition of the shaping power of the perennial rhythms and movements of Canadian nature. When this kind of knowledge is joined with that of the old man in the school, the result is a complete paradigm for the ancestral influences which structure our lives.

The "Eighth Letter" is a spirited, playful, and most inventive exercise in musical mythopeia. The "Second Letter" involved the putting of a vegetable form on Stratford; in the eighth the poet composes a musical form which uses several of the same basic images, beginning with the town's streets, this time played as scales, moving up and down with metronome-determined regularity and describing as they go such figures as "A Baptist minister walking up Nile Street" and "A truant officer on Romeo Street." Before this set of scales is finished we have been introduced to a rather cosmopolitan group of Stratford inhabitants, an Arabian girl, a French teacher, a Welshman, and an Irishman. The second set reveals an odd assortment of grocers and store keepers, including a seedsman who is "Fat as a well fed daffodil bulb" and twin grocers called Mr. Esau and Mr. Jacob who sell "rare First Editions of Kellogg's Cornflakes."

The scales are succeeded by a piece called "The Storm," played with the metronome set at a group of images almost straight out of Reaney's earlier poem "The Clouds": "at summer and pink and white and yellow brick sunlight with blue sky and white feather dumpling clouds." Out of this peaceful sky comes a sudden storm "With a windowpane shudder," bringing darkness into the library and umbrellas into blossom. After the rain-music the composition resolves itself on a delightfully fantastic sunset cadence of human joy after the storm:

> A cloud and a cloud and a cloudy
> Came out of the yellow garage.
> Joseph MacLeod in a many-coloured vest
> Danced to the Music dying in the west.

The most complicated sound effects are found in the Two Part Invention, played hands separately at first, until the pupil gets his bearings. Entitled "A Year in the Town," it is contrapuntal music for the changing seasons and proceeds, naturally, through four interweaving melodies: "The spring winds up the town"; "Frogs stop: put out the glass wind lantern / Tinkling summer on the porch"; "Crickets cry and the owl flies down / The ferris wheel and the fall rains fall"; "For three days no train or car got into the town. / The bakers had their yeast dropped from an airplane." Each seasonal melody is carried mainly in the right hand and has its left-hand accompaniment in a *Basso ostinato* or constantly accelerating repetition of basic "seasonable" images, "bud" for spring, "leaf" for summer, "twig and branch" for fall, and "blue and white" for winter.

The "Ninth Letter," called "Town House and Country Mouse," is a contrast between two worlds known to the Stratford poet, that of the farm, indicated by the phrase "Out here," and that of the town, designated as "there." Reaney's early attempt at a novel called *Afternoon Moon* is closer to this poem, in its imagery, its nostalgia, and its vivid sense of the vast distance between farm and small town, than anything in *The Red Heart*.[3] The dividing line between country and town is the highway

which succeeds the farm lane and the gravel road leading out
from the farm:

> On gravel now where corduroy logs from the past
> Look dumbly up
> Buried in the congregations of gravel,
> Getting closer the highway
> Cars darting back and forth
> In another world altogether.

The images here are closely determined by the actual locale,
now in the sixties only partly visible because of the combination
of urban sprawl and imminent rural slum filling the mile or two
between the Reaney farm and Stratford.

The country is defined in pastoral images of farm buildings,
sheaves of blue chicory, wild bees nesting, and a wild rose
bush. Then comes a half-world, neither country nor town, a
place of gas stations with windy signs, a slaughterhouse, orchards
gone wild, and drowned farms. To the eyes of the "Country
Mouse" the world of the town is a thing of terror and beauty:
"People turning and shining like lighted jewels," "one's first nun,"
"The first person with a wooden leg," "The swan." The device
of structuring the poem with the motif of a two-way buggy-ride
enables the poet to reassert the pastoral harmony of the country
against the bizarre shapes of the town; the return to the farm,
"Where barn is wedded to house," is described in terms of
backward looks at the receding half-world of the outskirts.

This Letter and the next two bring into the poem an element
of dread and grotesquerie familiar enough in Reaney's writings
as a whole but notably absent in Letters One to Eight. Throughout the shifting patterns and memorabilia of the whole book
the town of Stratford contains relatively little that is menacing
or too dissonant for the overall harmony of mood, but there is
in this Letter a suggestion of an even more perfect order of
reality than that of Stratford, comprehended by the life on the
farm. The terror felt by the boy in town, however, is mainly
one of delighted fascination, not the genuine, destroying fear
described, for example, with hilarity and pathos, in the Reaney
short story "The Bully."[4]

The "Tenth Letter" intensifies the use of unidealized, troubling
images. There is an old man with two canes and a white beard,
who walks along the road out of town with a huge sack on his

back. For some unexplained reason the poet is left disturbed and wondering about the stranger's identity. A sense of life gone wrong and of the human body in distorted forms can be seen in the description of Mr. Vermeer, "the specialist in trusses and supports" who lives "in a sorrowful red brick house" and has "two grave bespectacled kids / Eighty years old at the age of eight." It is also seen in the sad-faced boy in the street whose face is covered with whelks or the "evil red-haired boy" tormenting a girl and making her cry. These, and others, lead the boy observer into a nightmare in two parts, of the kind known to the Red Heart: about "a giant man dressed old" and coming down the street "with a clock in his belly"; about the christening shrouds of dead six-months babies reaching out at him from the church yard on the hill above the dam. Here again we have the perennial Reaney theme of children who are old men, of human life caught up in death's kingdom.

The "Shakespearean Gardens" described in the "Eleventh Letter" are Reaney's whimsical placing of the titles of sixteen of Shakespeare's plays so that they mirror the peculiar nature of Stratford, Ontario, as he sees it. Predictably, the Shakespearean forms fit oddly on the Canadian town but in each case a flash of ingenuity detects a parallel, physical or psychological, sometimes both. Of the physical sort we have the notation on *Othello:* "At the edge of town there stood a lonely white frame building—a deserted Negro church." The comment on *Macbeth* derives from amateur psychology: "Principal Burdoch's often expressed opinion was that a great many people would kill a great many other people if they knew for certain they could get away with it." Probably more interesting, even though left out of the radio version (presumably because it was thought too *recherché* for the public), is the entry for *King Lear:* "Mr. Upas was a silver haired cranky old individual who complained that the meat was too tough at the boarding house." The icon of the fabulous Javanese upas tree, whose poison kills all life for miles around, is just right for the silver-haired Lear who plunges a rational mind, a family, a kingdom, and a cosmos into turmoil, and yet, in his pettiness, complains about the table service. One further oblique connection between Shakespeare's art and the Canadian town which happened to get stuck with the name of Shakespeare's birthplace should be mentioned. It takes the form of a snatch of local conversation—*Troilus and Cressida:* "Well, I haven't been to that old Festival yet but since it began I've had ten different boyfriends."

The "Twelfth Letter" is at once a self-contained, movingly evocative lyric about adolescence and a poetic recapitulation of main images and themes from the whole suite. Called "The Bicycle," this poem identifies the time "Halfway between childhood & manhood" with a bicycle, "More than a hoop but never a car." The hoop, implicitly, symbolizes the self-contained unity and innocence of childhood; the car is explicitly associated with adulthood, sexuality, and destruction. The bicycle is a symbol of cyclical or wheel-like repetition and of upward ascent ("I climb on the stairs of my pedals"). As the former, it brings with it connotations of all the turning circular forms of the other poems— the spokes of the invisible wheel of the streets of Stratford, the bicycle-wheel feet of the white Twelfth of July charger, the life and the wallpaper repeating themselves in the house on King William Street, the wheels of the past "whirling in a fountain of sound at the place where the four branches meet," the old man and old woman revolving back to back, the ascending and descending scales of the music lessons, the ferris wheel and the red buggy wheels—all these and others come together in a poem intricately concerned with unity and harmony.

The other images to which the bicycle (adolescence) leads the poet are those of the road between home and the high school: "the bicycle talks gravel and rain pavement" and bears its rider past many of the sights mentioned in the preceding Letters. As the wheels turn, a year with its seasons revolves— "Autumn blows the windfalls down," "a secret robin is wintering," "The March wind blows me ruts over, / Puddles past, under red maple buds," "Fireflies tell their blinking player / Piano hesitant tales"—so that even dead frogs, burs, sharp wind, and swamp, images of malevolence in Reaney's earlier poetry, merge into a "world of love and of feeling / Continually floating down" on the soul of a poet whose "only knowledge" is of a harmonious reality held together by metaphor:

> everything was something,
> This was like that, that was like this—
> In short, everything was
> The bicycle of which I sing.

The spokes of the bicycle wheels are at once the branches of the town's streets and the branches of autumn in the piano lesson, blossoming out into asterisk shapes. These in turn are the stars, the wild roses, the fall leaves, and the character of the poet, as he cycles away from his childhood towards manhood, taking with him into his career as an adult poet the loved images of his homeland.

Twelve Letters to a Small Town, in its inspiration and even in some of its language, is reminiscent of Thomas's *Under Milk-Wood.* In its powerful feelings recollected in tranquility and in the poetic reality it constructs it draws extensively on a life in an actual place among real people. Still, the flexible shapes of a pastoral fantasia have transformed the historical facts into a structure of "pluperfect things" whose reality now belongs to the world of art.

CHAPTER 2

This Tottery Dance

I   A Suit of Nettles

A SUIT OF NETTLES is Reaney's longest single poem to date. Published in book form in the spring of 1958, it includes the author's suggestions for beginning an interpretation of it; there are fourteen quotations from widely different sources about geese, the ostensible subject of the book, a preface to the reader introducing the poem and giving some clues for background reading, and a few explanatory notes at the bottoms of the pages—making a total length of nearly 1700 lines. The book's publication, nine years after *The Red Heart* and four years before *Twelve Letters to a Small Town*, was greeted by several honors for the author, including the Governor General's Award for poetry, and by the poem's share of reviews in the usual Canadian places. There was also a review by Marie Ponsot in *Poetry* (Chicago). Among the reviewers the strongly favorable outnumbered the unfavorable by about two to one and it was possible, even that early, to see the outline of a sharp difference of opinion about this most bristling of Reaney's works.

On the one hand there was praise for the book's light satire, its complexity of interlocking imagery and themes, its technical bravura, and its poignant beauties. On the other hand it was indicted for being artificial, in a negative way, for uneasiness in its large metaphors, for pretentiousness, and for exasperatingly academic qualities. Munro Beattie, describing Canadian poetry between 1950 and 1960 for the *Literary History of Canada: Canadian Literature in English*, praised Reaney's "proficiency and versatility as a prosodist" but found his mind "completely innocent of satiric insight." And there the matter has rested, so far as any published discussion is concerned, although eight years have now elapsed since Reaney first asked the muse of

Satire to take Punch's stick and "Beat fertility into a sterile land." I should like to accept its prickly challenge and offer an interpretative commentary on it, as an intricately beautiful thing in itself, as a key production among the works of a writer who I think has some reasonable claim to being considered "a major literary figure," and as part of an ancient, very tenacious but never too familiar tradition of pastoral poetry.

A Suit of Nettles announces itself as an obviously and emphatically literary poem making use of highly stylized poetic conventions. It is a set of twelve pastoral eclogues, one for each month of the year, on the pattern of *The Shephearde's Calendar* by Edmund Spenser. The pastoral eclogue, despite the high degree of artifice involved in it, is a flexible form, technically and thematically. In its classical beginnings it was a short poem or part of a longer one, a "selection"; later the term was applied to bucolic or pastoral poems by Virgil. In the Renaissance it was made to serve satiric and allegorical purposes and to comprehend a wide variety of themes. In the eighteenth century, when town eclogues appeared, the term was applied simply to the form. In our century, Frost's "Build Soil," MacNeice's "Eclogue for Iceland," and Auden's "Age of Anxiety" show the form again being put into the service of the poet's social and political ideas. As used by Theocritus, Virgil, Petrarch, Boccaccio, and Spenser, the convention of the eclogue is one of humility, to be used by a poet before he is ready openly to declare his full powers.

Reaney's "Invocation to the Muse of Satire" indicates that his use of the form of the eclogue is primarily for satirical purposes. A reading of the whole poem, moreover, gradually reveals, eclogue by eclogue, how the purposes of satire are served by a well-defined romantic or pastoral myth. Those who know *The Red Heart*, with its curious mingling of irony and romanticism, will not find it surprising that this vastly more sophisticated and "curiously inwrought" book exploits the same two basic literary elements. The vision of innocence, however, has been expanded and unified while the contrasting vision of experience has deepened and intensified, to the point where each simultaneously illuminates the other. Later—in *Twelve Letters to a Small Town*, *Night-blooming Cereus*, "A Message to Winnipeg," *One-man Masque*, and *The Dance of Death at London, Ontario*—these two visions tend to separate again, the *Letters* and *Cereus* being dominantly idyllic and pastoral, the Winnipeg poem, the *Masque,* and the *Dance* nightmarish and satirical.

The pastoral world in literature is seldom presented as self-sustaining or secure; rather it normally appears to have within it the core of its own potential alteration. *A Suit of Nettles* is conventional in this respect also. It puts before us in an Ontario farm setting a representative society of geese (Canadians, human beings) who at the highest peak of their achievement compose lovely pastoral music and know of a high order of reality, but who are constantly threatened from within and without and who finally go down to nearly universal destruction. The choice of a rural Ontario world gives Reaney plenty of opportunity for description, often of a very literary sort, yet permeated with a personal knowledge of life on a farm in the 'thirties and an acute sensitivity to the colors, forms, and sounds of that life.

Like Chaucer's chickens, Swift's pygmies, and Apuleius's ass, Reaney's geese are a fantasy designed to break down customary mental associations and to precipitate a major shift in our habitual perspectives, in order to bring new life into the barren land of the Canadian mind. In the ludicrous fact of geese as central characters Reaney can give free play to his own poetic ambitions, cloaking in a suit of nettles his emotions and ideas; like Spenser he employs an eclectic method in the selection of forms and subject for treatment. The menologic idea aids this eclecticism by providing an easily adaptable pattern in which different aspects of the one poet's mind can gain expression. In the *dramatis personae* (the theatrical term is apt), Reaney can present beneath disguises, some of them very thorough but others more easily penetrated, himself and other people known to him in the culture in which he works. The goose characters, however, are not markedly realistic in any psychological sense. They are more like intellectual ideographs and have to be read as such.

II *"To the Reader"*

Reaney begins by establishing a wide range of connotations for the word "goose." After a dictionary definition giving "goose" in twelve languages, also the genus and a brief description of a goose as "usually larger than a duck, and smaller than a swan," we are plunged into an alphabet of goose lore extending from A to N and followed by "ETC," suggesting that this could go on and on. The alphabet is in the form of quotations from widely different sources, each one introducing into this most economical poem one or more ideas which later are to be relevant.

The first three—old Mother Goose wandering by riding through the air on a very fine gander, the gray goose and gander wafting the good king's daughter over the river, and "Goosey Goosey Gander where shall we wander"—indicate for the reader a movement out of his normal mental habitat into a world of fable, best approached by a child's imagination, in which geese play leading roles and even effect a human rescue. The idea of geese as timid or so stupid as to be easily beaten comes from the fourth entry, Macbeth's outburst at his servant early in the siege of Glamis: "The devil damn thee black, thou cream-faced loon! / Where gott'st thou that goose look?" From Sir Toby's instructions to Sir Andrew in *Twelfth Night* (III, ii) come two notions, that of a goosepen being an unlikely bearer of anything very bitter in its substance and that of the galling, irritating purpose of much of the writing involved in this book: "Let there be gall enough in thy ink, though thou write with a goosepen, no matter." A quotation from "The Story of the Inky Boys" in Heinrich Hoffman's *Struwwelpeter* brings into focus the figure of the very tall Agrippa, with mighty inkstand and great goosefeather, who serves in Hoffman's story as an agent of moral justice by dipping in black ink some boys who taunt a "blackamoor" for his blackness.

The contemptuous saying "What a goose you are" is connected by Reaney with the fact that in Egyptian hieroglyphics the emblem of a vain silly fellow is a goose. The distinguishing feature of hieroglyphics, as is well known, is that they are conventionalized pictures used chiefly to represent meanings that seem arbitrary and are seldom obvious. It may not be obvious that geese are the best emblem for unredeemed Canadian man but Reaney's poetic hieroglyphs are never entirely arbitrary. Certainly he works with what seem at first to be obscurities and far-fetched connections, but what he is doing is always saved, so far as communicability for the reader is concerned, by the pre-

cise observation forming the basis of the imaginative figure in
question and by the total sense gradually established by the
whole poem for each of its parts. No one could seriously expect
a Canadian poet setting out to write pastoral eclogues to depend
on sheep and shepherds for his emblems, and even the briefest
observation of an Ontario farm, back before mechanization and
specialization destroyed most of its variety and self-sufficiency,
would show that geese, among all the domestic birds and animals, were at once the silliest and one of the most various in
their usefulness.

Reaney's next hieroglyph is especially important. It helps
solve what looks like a serious problem in the use of geese as the
singers of pastoral music; geese can't sing. We are told that the
coat of arms of the Company of Musicians has on it a swan
with expanded wings within a double tressure, counter, flory,
argent and that this is perverted into a goose striking the bars of
a gridiron with its foot. The emblem, then, is called both "The
Swan and the Harp" and "Goose and Gridiron." The dust
jacket of *A Suit of Nettles* informs the reader that the book's
title was inspired by a German fairy tale (it is one of those collected by the brothers Grimm) in which seven suits of nettles
are woven by the sister of seven brothers who have been
changed into swans. When it is time for the brothers to resume
human form by putting on the suits, the arm of one suit is unfin-
ished and one brother always has one swan's wing instead of an
arm. The point about the geese (Canadians) is that they are
really swans, if they will put on their best selves and forsake
their perverted forms. They, like swans, can also sing rare and
beautiful music as they go to their deaths, and a select few of
Reaney's do.

The German tale, then, makes possible a theme of necessary
metamorphosis at the heart of the poem's satire, the same idea
associated by both Spenser and Yeats with the swan image. In
Spenser's "Ruines of Time" a swan suddenly appears in a cloud
of transfiguration and ascends into heaven, "Where now he has
become a heavenly sign; / There now the ioy is his, here sorrow mine." In the "Prothalamion" the "two gentle knights" who
are to marry the ladies Elizabeth and Katherine Somerset are
"two Swannes of goodly hewe" linked with one of the incarna-

tions of Jove himself who came to Leda in the form of a swan. In Yeats, as Reaney points out in Chapter II of his doctoral dissertation[1] (written in the same period as *A Suit of Nettles*), swan and water symbolize the two opposing states of consciousness. The swan is fire, and like the soul leaves the waters of emotion and passion in which all but purified souls are entangled. The separation of soul and body, of antithetical and primary, involves another start of the cycle that brings with it the rough beast slouching toward Bethlehem. For Yeats, then, the swan is the solitary soul, shown in the troubled, reflecting waters before it leaps into the desolate heaven: "That image can bring wildness." This kind of symbolism, involving necessary spiritual ascent from the world of sweet love and change, is of central importance for the story of Branwell, the protagonist, and his companions in *A Suit of Nettles*.

An excerpt from a Renaissance description of London tells us that "In the times of popery" there were eighteen whore-houses on the Bankside licensed by the Bishops of Winchester and that the whores therefore were called "Winchester Geese." This prepares for the Jezebel figure of "The January Eclogue," for the fair but faithless Dorcas, and also, perhaps, for the libidinous activities in the haymow above the goose society. We notice, however, that this kind of goose has a recognized function and is therefore sanctioned to some extent in the overall context. Next, Byron is quoted as an authority for seeing polite social activity in goose-terms: "For good society is but a game, 'The royal game of Goose,' as I may say" (*Don Juan*, Canto 12, 460). Byron in turn, although Reaney does not mention it, is quoting Oliver Goldsmith's *The Deserted Village*, line 232. The subsequent hieroglyph cites the sixteenth-century euphuist and satirist Thomas Nashe as saying, "Galen might *goe shooe* the Gander for any good he could doo. . . ." The classical Galen's authority in anatomy and physiology was virtually undisputed until Nashe's century (at this time the Swiss physician Paracelsus opposed the humoral theory of disease), with the result that medical progress was impeded. The reference suggests, perhaps, that this is an oblique indication by Reaney that his stance as satirist is that of the inconoclast, aware that something soundly based in the realities of belly, heart, and mind is needed, if any cure is to be effected in the society he is asking the Muse of Satire to cure of its sterility.

The last two entries in the goose alphabet have to do with the most obvious human use for geese, after their satirical potential is gone: "Christmas is a-comin' and the geese are getting fat." On the literal level this is where *A Suit of Nettles* concludes. The last entry, a quotation from Smollett, tells of the magnitude (up to two pounds) of Ferrarese goose livers which, however exquisite, were fed by the Roman Emperor Heliogabalus (Marcus Aurelius Antoninus) to his hounds. There would seem to be two reasons for this reference. Most obviously, the connection is with the farm people stuffing themselves at Christmas dinner in "The December Eclogue." Also, presumably, the reader is being promised a rich feast.

One is clearly not expected in a first perusal of *A Suit of Nettles* to puzzle over the hieroglyphs of the goose alphabet until each connotation has been tracked down, since the specific connections of the alphabet with what follows can fit into place only as one proceeds. The reader is expected, though, to do two things—to recognize the riddling, cryptic style of much of the writing in the book, and to perceive that the poet has, in his choice of geese as central symbol, struck out a very broad cultural territory as the content of his poem.

With the preface "To the Reader," hieroglyph gives way to almost equally abstruse suggestion parading as discursive prose, a sort of beginner's list of things to keep in mind while reading. We are reminded of the characters, story, themes, and poetic genres which make up *The Shephearde's Calendar*, and we are introduced briefly to the names of Reaney's geese, including the protagonist Branwell. We are also told that "The Church satirized in *A Suit of Nettles* is that defined by Coleridge as comprising all the intellectual institutions of the age." Then follows a list of cultural happenings—in the English literary world, in the U. S. A., in Canada, and in the Western world generally—which have caught the interest of the poet and made their way into the various eclogues.

There is also here an indication that the time reference of *A Suit of Nettles* is epic in its scope, extending, so far as Ontario is concerned, from the time of the glaciers till now, and, as regards the Western world, at least back to the ancient Irish bards. Further on in the poem this latter point in time is pushed even further back. Finally, and most important for the imaginative world created in the poem, through a combination of miniaturist artifice and mythopeia the poet tells us that the setting is a farm in Ontario with forty-three fields, the counties shown on an Ontario map. Even before *The Red Heart* Reaney had marked out this particular geographical area as the one which was to be the provider of raw materials in his construction of what in this book I call "Reaneyland," and had shown very early that his treatment was to be both pastoral and satirical. With *A Suit of Nettles* this particular imaginative space has been made vastly more inclusive, having pragmatically taken into itself, in theory at least, the whole of the history of Western culture.

III   *"Invocation to the Muse of Satire"*

The Invocation is in four stanzas, giving respectively the physical attributes of the Muse of Satire, a description of what she is to do, a briefer description of the sterile land which she enters, and a short anticipation of the result for the country cured by her. It is immediately evident that the poet's choice of a farm setting involves him in an exceedingly rich complex of images. The Muse emerges physically as a creature of piercing points, sharp edges, rottenness, and wintry cold. Aside from the fat phallus in her hand, borrowed by the poet from the old cover of *Punch* magazine, her other attributes are all rural. Each one is both a component part of her total anatomy and one in a series of metaphorical identities establishing her as a mythical being: her hands are of hawthorn branches in the winter, her teeth of cold March rain, her hair of bristly porcupines, her skin the mildewed skin of an ancient cow filled with botfly holes, her tears of ice, her eyes bright as the critical light on snow, her arms of gallows wood beneath the bark, her torso of a million hooked unhooking things, her legs of stainless steel knives and scythes, and her feet of harrows, with discs for shoes. She is, in short, a grotesque amalgam of those aspects of a farm which suggest violent and purposeful penetration. Her function is therapeutic, her way of working an incongruous parody of seduction. Each of her physical parts is to be brought into lacerating contact with the corresponding parts of the ones she embraces, the inhabitants of the sterile land.

The mauling to be given by the Muse is designed to be a physical, emotional, and mental anatomizing—"hour-long explorations / Of their life and heart and mind-line"—all with the purpose of restoring fertility in each of the three aspects of human life. The assault is described as primarily sexual, working through the senses, and comes to its climax when the dismembered phallus (a stick barbarously cut from a vine "of which new ones spring ever") has been beaten about the ears of the dead people until they have brought forth "something" and the phallus has burst into blossom.

The Doomsday theme of several of *The Red Heart* lyrics returns, now put to purposes of regeneration instead of being left simply an ironic statement of coming annihilation. The images are biblical and traditional—"make the sky red with doom and axey wrath"—and the fiction is meant to serve as the powerful medicine of satire. Despite the palpable qualities of the images, there are two indications that spiritual growth and transformation are the main overall aim. It is the heads of the inhabitants which are to be beaten and the land which has undergone the Muse's cure is described as one in which, like newly emergent moths leaving their "usual, foul and dark cocoons," the people who formerly have lived inside upturned privies now crawl forth in astonishment into a new order of being. The Invocation, then, defines the problem as one of sterility, suggests as cure a thorough satirical treatment, and looks forward to a life not known before.

IV *The January Eclogue*

Spenser's "January Eclogue" has as its zodiacal sign Aquarius the Water-Bearer, Aquarius having been the butler of the gods who gave them a waterpot. Reaney's "January" focuses attention on the wintry pond on the farm and on the question of whether or not Old Brown the farmer should break open the waterhole with his crowbar, thus letting the farm animals have water so that life may continue. On this symbolic base the Eclogue is constructed in the form of a conversation between two of the geese, Branwell and Mopsus, on the subject of love as it relates to geese and on the question of "whether they and all and life should cease." It is Branwell, crossed in love and wearing the green tatters of his suit of nettles, who seeks philosophical guidance from his friend Mopsus. Mopsus replies at length, making a strong recommendation that Branwell adopt the brotherly Platonic form of love and thus transcend all sensuality and "foul mad disorder." Branwell's rejection of Mopsus' plea for loyalty to "all that is unphysical" leads logically in the following months into much of the mental and physical action of the poem. As we shall see later, Branwell's decision is in some ways the right one, made for inadequate reasons.

Where Branwell is melancholy, Mopsus is splenetic, a thoroughgoing misanthropist and misogynist. In his long didactic speech he sets before Branwell caricatures of the major views of love in the Western world, the romantic idealization of eros, the Calvinistic loathing of sexuality, and the Platonic ideal of rational love. The first of these has its emblem in the figure of Jezebel, a combination of the mammalian females of some of *The Red Heart* poems and Reaney's later creation Madam Fay, as well as others; she tempts man "down a well of luscious shame" which simply "lugs" into the world another funeral. Mopsus' view of the sex act and conception is that of the Red Heart child made more prurient. He draws in the dung for Branwell a picture of man, a distorted, wet, groaning, hissing, and jerking horror whose one attraction is toward propagation. In his iconography, as in that of the Church Fathers and the mad Lear, the female pudenda are the mouth of hell. He despises the kind of physical union he has just overheard taking place up in the peastraw loft between Ann and the hired boy because he does not think that a man can love a woman for her soul. The love towards which he aspires will make no use of "This stake and heart-of-vampire sexual eye of ooze."

The "devil" Jezebel has her equally demonic antithesis in a Calvinistic Elijah figure whose effect is to overwhelm the individual with his own foulness until he inhabits a hell of despair and terror from which there is no means of ascent. He "gelds you from the world with sermons frore" only to turn you over to

worlds of dire
Pathless woods of rungless Jacob's ladders
Set in hollows filled with aspen-voiced adders.

From the lurid hells of Jezebel and Elijah, Mopsus calls Branwell to his "ferny groves by calm canals / Where all is bland, correct and rational," where one investigates "what one can't believe," and from which one finally gladly departs into "the new unbodied time" of eternal forms. Once man is "certain of the soul's affection," in Mopsus' understanding of existence, he has nothing to do with the terrestrial order of things but basks instead in the Light which severs the Sun from the planets. Branwell recoils at a light which never falls on the nine sick planets, finding it like a cold and dismal sea with no island to bring relief; he resolutely chooses "The world's hot middle where it's he and she," the world in which he wears "feverish stinging clothes." He even agrees that Mopsus' favorite land is better, but it is "a round concrete continent of snows," "too round and too continent" for him. As protagonist of the poem, Branwell rejects abstractions to stay in a world in which he can live through the cycles of human and natural life:

> . . . I want offspring summerson autumnman wintersage
> And tricklerrain thawwind panetap upleaf windrage
> Plow and seed and hoe, green, sucklepig, yellowripe,
> sicklestraw and all such glamourie.

The imagery and themes of this Eclogue draw on a wide range of sources, in addition to Reaney's knowledge of an Ontario farm. Most important, probably, is the beast fable convention whereby domestic fowl discuss philosophical and theological questions in the midst of their "human" problems. As in *The Nun's Priest's Tale*, where Pertelote refers to Chauntecleer's beard, we are not allowed to forget the dual perspective of the fiction; Branwell says to his friend, "You there, old Mopsus, you're no bird. / I see distinctly limbs beneath the feathers." The allusive quality of the diction supports the broad cultural reference of the major themes. There seems to be a broken echo in Branwell's "You've got a voice too that was never heard / Just in springtime" of "A voice so thrilling ne'er was heard / In springtime from the cuckoo bird." Phrases like "these green tatters" and "Crossed in love" have a Shakespearean resonance, and Mopsus' expression for the impossibility of finding heaven through sexual love—"More jumping in and out of needles' eyes"—is an ironic twisting of a well-known New

Testament text. There is an Old Testament reference in "You say you love through girl her elohim." The line "More love poems, paradoxes, happy unions, lies" embraces a vast body of romantic literature on erotic themes and Mopsus' brotherly love clearly has a special affinity with that of Socrates for Alcibiades in *The Symposium.* Also working here are the ancient idea of the world of the Sun versus the world of the cave and shadows, the medieval theory of the four humors, and the traditional idea of the four ages of man.

Reaney's "January," like the rest of *A Suit of Nettles,* does not depend for its accessibility on a knowledge of Spenser's *Shephearde's Calendar.* On the other hand, such a knowledge does add an extra dimension, since Reaney's pastoral is a deliberate and conscious attempt to recreate in a Canadian environment the vision of Spenser's poem. There are close similarities in Branwell's position as one disappointed in love and that of Spenser's Colin, who has been rejected by Rosalinde. Each protagonist is wooed by a male friend who prefers, in E. K.'s words, the love of the "soule" to that of the "person." The description of January weather is more extended in Spenser and identified more completely with the lover's melancholy. The "barrein ground" is a "myrrhour" in which Colin beholds his plight, paralleling Reaney's use of "the two-faced time whose sun no more goes south" as objective correlative for Branwell's feelings. Also like Spenser, Reaney includes archaisms (the Scottish and northern dialect word "drouth," the Old and Middle English "frore," and the Sir Walter Scott "glamourie") and paronomasia or puns ("continent," "offspring," "summerson," "autumnman," "wintersage"). The stanzaic form of Reaney's "January," "February," and "March" is a close relative of the Spenserian stanza; containing four rhymes, it is composed of nine decasyllabic "heroic" lines followed by an Alexandrine which rhymes with line nine. There is a pronounced tendency, however, to let a four-beat accentual meter dominate: "Hís teeth against hér teeth with skúll ténsion."

V   *The February Eclogue*

"February" is firmly located in the mutable world of natural cycles chosen by Branwell at the end of "January." The overall theme of the poem, fertility versus sterility and death, is developed in three distinct but interrelated areas, the history of Ontario, Branwell's love, and the conflict between muscle and poetry in Canadian society. Against an abstract mythical pattern of a life-begetting and masculine solar principle and a life-bearing and feminine lunar one, the cycles of human, animal, and goose birth and death are described in a passage of finely conceived metaphors. The close correlation of conception and death which pervades much of Reaney's early writing is still here but is now stripped of the earlier tendency to take delight in negation of life:

> The young cub forms like a dim loose star-knot
> In the lioness as down the sun sets,
> Night wobbles in, and spirit goslings sought
> To dance this month through the small small eyelets
> Of birth before birth, death before death pinned
> Resolved & tight in each large goose egg's centre inned.

In the figure of new spirits dancing through the eyelets of birth, we have the subtle reply to Mopsus' "More jumping in & out of needles' eyes" in "January." In a beautifully fresh use of an old symbol for resurgent natural life Reaney identifies a crowing rooster so closely with the rising sun that it is impossible to say whether "it" in the following lines has its antecedent in "throat" or "sun":

> "Occurocceroo," crowed Thompson the cock,
> His small throat tied fast to the giant sun
> Kicking aside the night as it rose. . . .

The theme of Canadan (especially Ontario) history is introduced with the return to the gooseshed of the "pretty girl" goose Dorcas who has been recovering from a broken leg in the farmhouse. While there, in her basket under Quebec (a note by the poet explains the simple two-fold allegory of this—Quebec is a kind of stove and is also the province above Ontario on a map), she has gleaned a knowledge far beyond "a goose's wildest nightmares." She recounts this knowledge in two ways, in an imagistic description of the details of the farmhouse and in an allegorical reading of the events of Ontario history, these two being the first extended introduction into the poem of the contrast between the superficially attractive aspects of the farm world and the darker reality of bloodshed and horror underlying it.

The account of the farmhouse once again emphasizes the strength of Reaney's attachment to the farmhouse in which he spent his childhood. It is the still center from which several of his most powerful and pervasive symbols emanate. Whatever thematic use he makes of it in a particular poetic context, it is always palpable, intimately known, and filled with wonder and mystery. Dorcas too has fallen victim to its spell and her sojourn there stays in her mind as "that dear gold time" when her mistress bade her play on the piano "softer than a dove" or climb on top of the table and watch the eight-day clock.

There is plenty, however, that is ominous in this habitation, and even the intellectually limited Dorcas, whose view of reality is completely circumscribed by clocktime, historical events, and narcissistic self-absorption, has penetrated through the guilty layers of the wallpaper and come to know of the slaughter of forest and Indians which went into the house's construction. She gives a goose's-eye view of the élitist world of the "first son" of the farm family (the Family Compact), who played cards and went to "proper-church" (the Anglican, of course), and of the "second son," William Lyon Mackenzie, who "did plot beneath a beer vat much."[2]

The farmhouse still has scratches on the floors "Where brothers fought" (the rebellion of Upper Canada) and "where distant relatives / Once stormed the place and roasted all the doors" (the War of 1812 with the U. S. A.). But Dorcas takes the conventional view of Canadian history; after the "once-possessing natives," that is the Indians, had been subdued, there was no grand excitement up until the time of World War I, when the lives of all the males "were risked in thresh-machine." The war-dominated world since then, with all its demonic fascination with the means of annihilating human life on a grand scale, is ironically summed up by Dorcas in images of Canadians destroying forests or stooking grain and harvesting it: "They chop down trees to build a gallows with; / Machines they build to thresh their gathered sons to death." Dorcas finds the stupid utilitarian narrowness and the ongoing destructiveness charac-

teristic of much in Canadian life just like that of herself and
her fellow geese:

> But the people living here are yet much
> Like us: brick upon brick—they are new born,
> They grow up, earn a living, learn prudence,
> Depress a bed, beget a blockhead; mourn—
> For the next brick seals them down, down, down, down.

The farmhouse is shown to be a superficially appealing wallpapered illusion. Within it, far more powerful than any of the
petty historical events which make up its life, "an ancient voice
the silence steals," drowning out the heart-beat and skull-hum
of the present inhabitants and recalling a time of primordial beginnings when nature was the one seen by the bird which
hovered over the new creation in Genesis 1 and was seen again
just prior to Noah's emergence from the ark. "Take us back to
our beginnings, white sail shipbird, / Uncut this forest old and
our old countries green." Strange birds in Reaney's symbolism
usually announce a new cycle, a movement from one ring of
time into another. Here the impulse is retrospective, based on a
sense of things having once been better, in what Mircea Eliade
would call *in illo tempore.*

Branwell's love centers on Dorcas, the prettiest goose in the
shed, who, for all her knowledge of history, is a traditional icon
of self-love and fatal, ensnaring beauty. She sits off in a corner
by herself "with her glass / Primping & being admired by all"
and her character is one of "melting shifty vows." Branwell,
ludicrously smitten, pays elaborate homage to his *femme fatale,*
with a jews'-harp serenade, a song in the form of a sestina, and a
"sparkling pretty rose diamond ring." The whole sequence is a
parody of courtly love conventions, an exercise in bathetic art
and a display of the poet's technical skill.

Dorcas is celebrated according to her six most beautiful
features, her "blue eyes intense as salt," the sounds that from
her beak "do spring," her "swift beak," her "paddling legs,"
her stainless white mind, and her feathers like snow. She is a
"dread white goddess," a white angel, and Branwell is totally
inferior, slow-witted and filled with dread. Two key words
run through the six stanzas and the envoy, "worth" to denote

her excellence and "grime" his unworthiness. According to the courtly pattern, he offers abject flattery, adoration to the point of idolatry, and undying service if she will show mercy and redeem him, but Dorcas also is true to the convention; she has already given herself to someone else and spurns her would-be suitor. The contrast between the elevated style used by Branwell and the commonplace goose romance described, runs through the sestina and comes to its climax in Dorcas' throwing Branwell's ring back at him, then laying a large white egg fathered by the shambling "chop-the-harp and fish-with-the-strings-sort of oaf," George. The esthetic, idealistic Branwell, whose purgatorial experiences sound like an Elizabethan sonnet sequence, meets his antithetical self in the muscular, virile, and completely non-intellectual George.

Branwell's tragic rejection is followed by an uproar in the gooseshed equal to that in the poor widow's yard when daun Russell seizes Chauntecleer. Mopsus realizes that the ring offered Dorcas is the one he has given Branwell; in hurt rage he knocks down the suffering youthful poet, who is then kicked by George and abused, in a *Rape of the Lock* sort of couplet, by Dorcas: "Beneath me girls you see a dying swan; / Beside me view a goose: which race would you breed on?" For "a goose" read "real he-man" and the point about the fate of the despised intellectual or artist is clear. Mopsus' loyalty reasserts itself and he nearly throttles Dorcas, then attacks George. From there all the geese get involved, "A big muscular stout hot gander mob" against the poetry lovers, who are nearly defeated until there emerges a goose called Raymond, who is both muscular and poetic and has his historical counterpart in the Ontario farm poet Raymond Knister.[3] The mock-heroic battle is ended not by a sudden return of rationality, as in Chaucer, but by the timely arrival of Ann to feed the geese.

VI *The March Eclogue*

By the beginning of "The March Eclogue" Branwell has regressed badly. The sight of Effie (who now emerges as a major figure in the poem), "lively as a wind-up toy" and turning the goose eggs to keep them from addling, fills him with disgust. The severe shock he has experienced in "The February Eclogue" has led him to adopt the view of sex and reproduction taken by Mopsus in "January" and by the Red Heart child (it simply permits "scores of new cherubs" to be plunged into the hell of existence) and to abnegate the "glamourie" of the world of nature. Now a figure of disillusionment and melancholy, he tries to convince Effie that the cruelty shown her by her mother, after she had been a dutiful and devoted daughter for ten years, should be sufficient proof that love is founded on dreams and doomed to fail, whereas Hate is the reality and rules supreme. He has adopted a completely "sublunary" view of existence (Hate "is what rules fire earth air and sea"), the logical but destructive consequence of the nature-worship which underlies his female-worship.

In "February" Dorcas has set before the other geese a vision of an artificial, time-dominated, and illusory farmhouse world receding as a mysterious voice speaks from a point at the beginning of mythical time. Now in "March," Effie brings into the poem the first of several glimpses of a genuine pastoral reality to set against the world of Branwell's suffering. It is significant, though, in terms of the *mythos* of the whole poem, that the ideal is presented tentatively at this point, in terms of seeming and dreams. She calls up, from her own and Branwell's childhood memories, an apprehension "of somewhere else / Than water earth and air and fire," the elements that now seem to be their whole universe. She once experienced a visionary dream of "a white walled garden" in which a Blakean child "sat playing on a panpipe" made of "twinkling golden straw." This child explained to her that the beauty and grace of the pipe came from its having been "cut from a farm / In which our universe of stars is but a stone / Sulking in fields of dew it cannot see." This vision of a lost but eternal paradise has stayed with her because she took her heart "and opened it / To better hear his strange glad minstrelsy." It permits her to live in but not of the world of "ingratitude and dread, / Rage, boredom and soul-starving deficit."

Effie's vision of eternal forms parallels that of Mopsus but is qualitatively different; it concerns a place where physical things are transformed, not rationalized away into abstractions, and it leads to a love of life and human potential in this world, not to aversion and contemptuous cynicism: "You must not sneer; this egg may hatch a heart / That will not close itself against a golden dart." Effie spiritually inhabits a higher order, the one from which the golden sun-lover came down as a "trapped yellow wanderer" to live in the dungeon of the Red Heart. The narrative movement of "The Heart and the Sun," however, and that of Effie's story are different; in the earlier poem an eternal form enters time only to depart, leaving behind a dead human body, while for Effie an early knowledge of paradisal oneness remains with her in the changeful fallen world of adult experience.

But Branwell's heart, at this point, is not opening to any vision from the kingdom of the sun. He too *has* a "dream" (he uses the present tense where Effie used the past), a nightmare not a vision, in which he is surrounded by the moon in all her phases, "twenty-eight silvery pock-faced whores" who spin round him, turning all his grasping for "what seems young" into "what's old." The practical result has been to destroy completely his former intellectual pleasure in "grasping / Difference and likeness" and to provide a containing metaphor for everything he sees; robin, rose, sunset, geese, winds, and weather all have taken on the form or aspects of a rat. Even in a mental landscape as twisted as this, something antithetical intrudes to prevent the sulking youth Branwell from being entirely lost: "Sometimes a nest of angels in the sun steal in my eyes like thieves." But he banishes them, by rolling on the ground in his suit of nettles. It seems, then, that at this point in the poem the suit of nettles, formerly symbolizing what it is to be alive in the world of the passions and nature, has now become a willful insistence on being wretched and on sinking into a complete nothingness. As in Yeats, to be moon-dominated is to be caught in the welter of private emotions.

Branwell has abandoned all attempts to see either differences or identities but Effie shows herself a reconciler of opposites ("our dreams are quite alike you know") and proceeds to show how her white wall is Branwell's circling moons, her garden the glade in which he sees "a dying world," and Branwell himself "the fallen heir" of her "piping child." Out of this synthesis comes, by implication, the first important cure for the "land with spires and chimneys prickly" described in the Invocation, the "foul mad disorder" seen by Mopsus in "January" and the "guilty house" in "February." Effie explains the problem as she sees it; the dark, moon-destroyed world has "lost its lore / Of weaving into charms that shine a star." Her images are apocalyptic, having to do with imaginative conquest and control of the apparent irreconcilables of a life in nature and history: "Nail whirlwinds and make spades of swords of war, / Raise up the dead. . . ."

To further explain her view that Branwell's world is simply one in which imaginative energy has failed, so that creativity, vision, redemption, and resurrection no longer are believed in, Effie tells "a curious tale" about a Doorknob and a Door which turns out to be one of the most enigmatic passages in *A Suit of Nettles*.[4] The Doorknob is "white and rather poor, / Yet handy" while the Door is made "of solid pine, / Dark brown and varnished slick and fine." In his superbity the Door attacks the Knob as a "pale weak thing" spoiling the look of him the "king," by making him asymmetrical. This leads the Knob into two long, difficult speeches which must be understood if an important part of the symbolism of the poem is not to be missed.

The Knob talks of three things: the sound of the Door's voice; the contrast between the humble daytime work of the Knob and the turbulent nighttime dreams he experiences; the dire results for Door and Knob of the Door's rage. With the first of these there is no particular problem; the Knob is puzzled by what the Door is and gropes towards a definition of him, with the help of two analogies: the Door's voice "is like the sound of snow / Heard in mind of summer rainbow, / Or dumb seedless lumps of dark zinc / When green leaves try to on them think." In view of the poem's wider theme of wintry sterility versus fertility, and also of the enigmatic use shortly of the Noah myth, the Knob would seem to be telling the Door that he belongs to those antithetical forces of darkness which hold back emergence of a new creation under the promise of the rainbow. Similarly, there is no potential life in "dumb seedless lumps of dark zinc" when "green leaves" (living things, the Knob, those in nature who wear a suit of nettles) try to comprehend them. These are only approximations, the Knob knows, to a definition of the Door's nature, but he knows also, with precision, what is his own daily function in relation to the Door; he is to think and "size up each approaching hand / And fit it with a surface bland."

The Knob's dreams are destroying sea-beasts—Whales of Lust, Rays of Hate, Madness like Eels, Fear like Skate—who "Swim rough and tumble" in his mind, devouring his sanity but also warning him what equipment he must choose if he is to travel safely through the next day's sea voyage. The choice is determined by the nature of the enemies, which may require nets, hooks, trident, leaden shoes, harpoons, or cages. Earlier in this Eclogue Effie has shown us her vision of paradise. Now, in the fable which she tells to Branwell and Mopsus, we see the dark antithetical reality which underlies the individual soul seeking, in the Knob's words, to "learn for climbing world-life's street." *A Suit of Nettles* is a poem about mental or spiritual travel imagined as taking place in an upwards spiraling movement, at any point of which lust, madness, hate, and fear threaten to impede or stop the progress. Dorcas' rejection of Branwell has, at least for now, stopped him. The cyclical world he resolutely chose in "January" contains the soul-destroying beasts and emotions inside man which must be understood and controlled if the individual is to travel "through clouds of thoughts & hands," that is, perform his intellectual and physical work.

The Door, of course, dumb seedless lump that he is, understands nothing, and so, like all who prefer brute ignorance to insight, he is enraged by this display of deep thinking on the Knob's part. Convulsed and shaking he breaks the Knob in two and the noise wakes farmer Smith, his wife, and his five sons. In a scene of wild rough-and-tumble farce the Door is "Crazed into splinters" and the Knob becomes a children's toy in the farmhouse. Effie finishes her fable with a curious statement about the Knob becoming a kind of mentor for the farmer's children:

> Still thinking, dreaming, showing them
> How to be Ham, Japhet and Shem
> And drunken Noah as all men must
> Who for the height of being lust.

Mopsus is bewildered ("Ham, Shem, Drunken Noah? What does it mean?") and Branwell has "felt" the meaning in his heart even though as yet his "rusted mind" has not understood. He is aware that the experience he has just had is "a knot" which "logic fingers" cannot ravel out at once. Mopsus is fascinated and will not sleep a wink until he has understood what the sibylline Effie has meant. He recognizes that she has some power of divination and so urges her to accompany them to Mome Fair to explain the merry-go-round, the ferris wheel, and the sideshows, all of which projects the reader's attention forward to "The September Eclogue."

Before going on to "April" let us recall those pieces of Reaney's puzzle already in place. In the midst of a sterile land sits a gooseshed with its various inhabitants. One of them has denied the reality of this physical place while another clings to it and to his love for its prettiest inhabitant. A third lives in the goose-shed world according to an inner music emanating from a belief in an eternal order beyond. She tries to instruct the other two on how to live wisely in the lower order while progressing spiritually to the higher. By the end of "March" her teaching is well begun but the two disciples are as yet very much novices.

This simple narrative plot has, to this point, involved several episodes of an underlying myth which provides resonance and poetic richness as well as the beginnings of an abstract shape for the whole poem. In the hieroglyphs geese were mentioned as wandering and, in one rhyme, as rescuing "the good king's daughter." The Invocation, as we noted, contains the Doomsday theme and biblical images of wrath and judgment, which connect up with the Jezebel and Elijah "devil" figures of "January" and the hells they lead people into, as well as with the blood-guilt of the farmhouse described by Dorcas, in which an ancient voice steals the silence and calls for a return to primordial beginnings through the help of a "white sail shipbird." It seems that the maturing of the wandering and confused Branwell and of Mopsus must involve recognition of the informing power of the ancient biblical story of man's journey through a barren land or chaotic sea back to God. Once Branwell has begun to see that he is wrong (or, at the very least, sure to be disappointed), when he calls Dorcas his "white angel in bethlehems of grime," he is in a position to begin travelling towards a real Bethlehem. Effie has presented him and Mopsus with the Doorknob as a handle to hang on to while they think the matter through, as a sort of Noah's ark which will save them temporarily from believing in the victory of hatred while they prepare to aspire to "the height of being." We remember that it is the Sibyl in Virgil's epic who provides the protagonist entering the underworld with a protective golden bough.

VII   *The April Eclogue*

"The April Eclogue" takes the form of a "bardic contest in honour of Spring" between two geese called Raymond (for Raymond Knister) and Valancy (for Isabella Valancy Crawford) and judged by a third goose called Duncan (Duncan Campbell Scott).[5] The singing contest ends in a draw when the fictional judge cannot decide which competitor has won, meaning that if a decision is to be made it is up to the reader. Appropriate to the celebration-of-spring theme of the Eclogue and to the larger theme of the poem, the prize is a kernel of the hardest winter wheat.

Where Spenser's "April" includes a long lyric in praise of Elisa, the fair queen of shepherds all, Reaney's, through Raymond, celebrates the earth as a great black goddess, and, through Valancy, as a sleeping beauty called awake by the panegyric in her honor. Raymond's theme of the fertility of the earth leads him through a series of strikingly similar metaphors for the goddess: a black sow huge with birth, a black ogress who ate her glacier lover, a black begum of a thousand dugs. The myth of mother Earth is of course archetypal, joined here to Reaney's knowledge of the emergence of the landscape of Ontario at the time of the recession of the glaciers (the sun killed Earth's lover for her)[6] and to the Noah myth, as birds and animals ("Caw caw whir whir bark bark") emerge from the Ark at the time of this new creation. Ontario's Indian past is associated with the timeless migrations and continuing life of the wild goose: "Wild geese come in arrowheads / Shot from birds long ago; / Buried in your negro snow." In a series of Knister-like images for springtime activity on the farm there is an echo of the earlier war-versus-creative-work theme of "Feb-

ruary": "Mr Sword or Mr Plow / Can settle in your haymow."
In her endless fertility the goddess is mother of all natural
things, including the poet himself:

> Great goddess I from you have come,
> Killdeer crow geese ditch leaf plowman
> From you have come, to you return
> In endless laughing weeping round.

Valancy's hymn to the earth is Reaney's poetic tribute to what
he understands and admires in the poetry of Isabella Valancy
Crawford, her tendency to see the Canadian landscape as half-
human, as potentially under human imaginative control. Where
Hobbinol in his encomium on Elisa used classical allusions mixed
with English landscape images, Valancy uses biblical ones
adapted to the Ontario landscape reviving in the spring. As the
winter of unbelief is pushed away, fanatic doves, believing
wrens and orioles and devoted redwinged blackbirds herald a
new incarnation in the forms of "all young things, all children,"
fathered by the sun on the earth which is both Eden and Bethlehem. The stanzaic pattern is a beautifully intricate nine-line
unit modeled on that of Colin's lyric sung by Hobbinol, a
skillful combination of long and short lines, of rhymes and
assonance, of soft feminine endings interchanging with masculine ones, all preceded by an italicized epigraph giving the basic
metaphor of the stanza:

> *Your limbs are the rivers of Eden.*
> From the dead we see you return and arise,
> Fair girl, lost daughter:
> The swallows stream through the skies,
> Down dipping water,
> Skimming ground, and from chimney's foul tusk
> Their cousins the swifts tumble up as the tusk
> Of roar day
> In bright May
> Scatters them gliding from darkness to sun-cusp.

VIII   *The May Eclogue*

By the time "The May Eclogue" begins, "the small small eyelets / Of birth before birth, death before death" pinned in the
centers of the goose eggs in "February" have become a flock of
goslings, "infant furry pocket suns," which Effie and Fanny pro-

tect against skunks, snapping turtles, and foxes; in Spenser's "May" a crafty fox devours a credulous kid and "many wyld beestes liggen in waite." The zodiacal sign for Spenser's Éclogue is Gemini "the Twins"; in Reaney's, Fanny tells her companion a story about two twins who completely outfox a pair of female experts in contraception. This is a rollicking near-doggerel handling, in a variety of poulter's measure, of the theme of what Whitman called "the great procreant urge of the world" triumphing over a deliberate and unnecessary sterility. There are several overtones which make it clear that the "sense of lively birth" championed here is associated with the large families of French Roman Catholic Canadians.

Fanny has heard that the "hill country" geese, who have big families of forty-two or fifty-two goslings, recently have been preached at for a year by "two strange geese of the scientific variety" who came to them bearing a great array of sterilizing objects—including a piece of straw, a frazzled bit of string, the old button from a castrati's overcoat—with which, they claimed, the women could ensure that they would have babies only by choice. The benefits cited are the usual ones, to a point—proper care of the children who are born and an easier life for the mothers—but Reaney's satire points up the underlying self-indulgence, even the perversion (as well as the Canadian Protestant's anti-Catholic prejudice), which frequently underlies strong championing of small families:

You then could buy yourself a kill-yourself-if-you-touch-it
And a watch-everybody-squeeze-up-from-hell-while-you-sit;
An electric jelly-fish warmer than a husband to go to bed with you
And a pass-like-a-vulture-shadow-and get your sons to do
Two-backed tricks in the back and flatten 5,000,000 frogs too.

(Non-Canadian readers may not be aware that "frogs" is a slang word of contempt for the approximately 5,000,000 French Canadians.) The two "smooth ladies" meet incomprehension in some places, the traditional arguments of Rome in others: the real answer is not artificially to limit childbirth, but to improve the standard of living of poor people; procreation is natural and good in marriage and it is sin to hate "being."

On the verge of leaving the community as failures the two ladies meet their nemesis in the form of "two handsome yet/ Sort of grim rakish sly curly young men who look just like" and have names full of punning suggestiveness to do with Catholic fertility and phallic powers, "Roderick" and "dreadful Benedict." These "strange men dark and wild" set up "a ceaseless mad tattooing / Of caresses" once they get the ladies into their house of many gables, "mossy roofed," "Set between leafy thick apple-tree rows." Despite the elaborate contraceptive measures taken by their spouses on the bridal night—here Reaney writes with fine excess—both are shortly pregnant:

They tied the brothers up in sheets of tight
Glass, beaten gold, cork, rubber, netting, stoppers, sand;
They themselves damned their wombs with a pretty skillful hand
And lay back waiting for the sensation
Of an interesting lively copulation. . . .

Having made the ladies bear with "The ripeness of a Nile," the brothers then turn them "into strong & sturdy machinery" for serving the purposes of seed-time and harvest; one becomes "a large squat fanning mill" (presumably for separating out the fertile grain from the chaff), the other "a tall conical cylindrical / Iron Maiden used for threshing seeds from ripe sunflowers." And so Fanny and Effie amuse themselves while seeing to it that goose-life continues.

IX   *The June Eclogue*

In "April" and "May" Branwell has been in the background. When he reappears in "June," talking to Mopsus, it is clear that the songs about the arable earth and Bethlehem and the description of hill country productivity have had no restorative effect on him. Spenser's "June" is "wholly ouwed to the complayning of Colins ill successe in his loue." The mood and theme, as well as the focusing on the lover and his friend, show a close correspondence to Reaney's Eclogue. It is in three parts: a lovely imagistic lyric by Mopsus about the perfection of a June day ("Humming blue gold air," "The wild rose opens simple eyes / In a green briar face," "The strawberry like a wren's heart"); descriptions by Branwell and Mopsus of birds; a song of despair by Branwell who "can't look like the time."

Branwell is completely wretched, but has been trying to raise himself out of his gloom by shooting with his gun at a bird that eats his sun, a hooting owl which he cannot kill and which blights "the fields' green hue / Into the gray of dream."[7] Mopsus understands because his father once had such an "edge-less, blurred" bird on his head but learned that he could not fight it. He just had to wait for its wrath to dissolve: "To fight that bird were downright folly / For her name is Melan-choly." To understand this is no help to Branwell, who has learned that Dorcas, while talking "betrothal" with him, has given all his gifts as well as her body to "that gross buck" George. Branwell's song of despair describes the emotional and mental metamorphosis he has undergone. He is like "a hollow tree / Dead in the forest of his brothers" and the pastoral music he "like a golden bird" once made has fallen silent. As he watches the sunset of the summer solstice ("I see the red sun sink / For the last time this far north"), he cries out for the bird of prey to leap from the "swampy fair" of his mind. Instead, the full moon rises and we recall that, earlier, Effie has tried to help Branwell escape from malign lunar influences into the kingdom of the sun.

X   *The July Eclogue*

In "June" we see the spiritual death which comes from the idolizing of a *femme fatale*. In the argumentative prose eclogue "July" we are shown, in the figure of a schoolmaster called Anser ("Goose"), the intellectual death which results from those so-called progressive theories of education which depend for their appeal on a fundamental inertia in the minds of the intellectually lazy and on the creation of a permissive atmosphere in which the "life situation" and what the child decides determine every-thing. With such a theory the laziest and most ignorant adults can be teachers and the child learns nothing disciplined or lib-eralizing. Anser's first word is "Hohum," his arguments are all clichés ("You cannot educate the young goslings by fear," "Let them be happy," "how useless so far as the actual living of life is concerned," "The self must be free"), and his pupils are so free that they have left the school altogether. Valancy, here a humor-ous caricature of the Canadian historian Dr. Hilda Neatby, who routed a progressivist on a CBC "Citizens' Forum," argues for the superiority of a more traditional kind of schooling.

Each side in the debate is associated with an obviously icono-graphic setting; Valancy as a pupil went to "the granite boulder in the pasture" but Anser has moved the school to a "boggy acre." Valancy's former teacher, Old Strictus, kept discipline and even resorted to physical punishment ("a strong thrumming dig of his old yellow beak"). His Spenserian connotations put him in line with the faithful shepherd Abel, with Moses, and with the apostles, all of whom tended their flocks as they should have. There is also a parallel in the goatherd Morrell's herd straying among the bushes rank and Anser's letting his goslings "steal into the fields of pease & buckwheat & gorge themselves to their heart's content." Most important, Old Strictus taught "the most wonderful list of things," which some of the poorer students did not succeed in learning until November, but when they did "they knew all that a young goose was supposed to know" and "it was as joyous a moment as if they had been reborn into another world." In response to Anser's sarcastic "Might I ask just what this reviving curriculum was?" Valancy explains. They learned "the children of the glacier and the earth," "the four elements," "the seven colours," "the ten forms of fire," "the twelve tribes of Israel," "the eight winds," "the Nine Worthies," and so on. Their studies even included "the stones that support New Jerusalem's wall." Anser is appalled, to the point of revealing the basic hopelessness and defeatism on which his own pedagogical theories are based, the kind of falsely utilitarian Doomsday view of the purposes of schools and universities which those of us who live in the post-Sputnik "freedom-loving-nations-against-the-Communist-tyranny" world know so well: "I mean since our heads are going to be chopped off anyhow we only teach the young gosling what he likes."

XI   *The August Eclogue*

It is clear from Reaney's post-January account of the progress of the goslings and of natural life in general, in the eclogues from "February" to the end of "July," that the problem of physical sterility has in an immediate sense been solved. It is also clear that, with a very few notable exceptions—Effie, Raymond, Val-ancy—the goose world contains individuals who are severely re-tarded in terms of their capacity for what Blake called "mental fight." "August" continues the satire on Coleridge's Church ("all the intellectual institutions of the age") by laying bare some of the mental habits of literary critics which bring death to the art of literary criticism, just as Anser's do to the minds and imaginations of the young who cannot look up to be fed by a faithless teacher because they aren't even in school.

Raymond happens upon the funeral of a famous goose-critic and is astonished to learn certain things about the critic and his attitudes to literature. During the proceedings the critic's ghost is raised by a judicious evaluating of three lyrics. When Terpsichore herself, the muse of the dance and of lyric poetry, objects to the proceedings, the disciples try to mutilate her. Fortunately, as Raymond points out, "noone can kill a Muse / Unless their own to kill they choose." The shade of Scrutumnus rises out of sulphur and Raymond notices that there is a spider in the critic's harp, suggesting, one supposes, that Scrutumnus and his disciples are almost as destructive in their impact on imaginative literature as the harp-smashing George. In Blake's symbolism, well known to Reaney, the spider is a symbol of the spectral, gloomy Selfhood.

"August" is exuberant intellectual parody of two things, the pastoral elegy or funeral poem, and the critical theory and practice of F. R. Leavis and his followers who made the journal *Scrutiny* famous. There is the conventional procession of mourners (disciples, muses, furies, graces, screeching owls, shrieking women with their dresses dyed black), the eulogy of the deceased (Scrutumnus contained in his wee head "A sharper sense of good and bad / Than all the ages' gooses had" and he preferred the music of copulation sung by pigs and sparrows to that of thrushes), the strewing of flowers (pigsweed and lambsquarters gone to seed), and even a parody resurrection accompanied by the smell of sulphur.

Three caricature samples of lyric poetry are recognized by Terpsichore as an illustration of how different poetic purposes result in different choices of language and style. Each is good in its own way. The first is about a pair of lover-pigs snorting and grunting "in the sties of Venus," illustrating the Jezebel love described earlier. This poem is greeted by long applause. In the second, a lover in euphuistic language addresses his lady and laments her preference for his "rival's golden bags." This poem, no less sexual than the first but dressed up with elaborate diction, receives moderate applause. It is not too dissimilar from Branwell's Petrarchan conceits. The third is Miltonic and Latinate and does not concern love; it is instead an invocation to a cherub, seraph, or angel for poetic inspiration. We can imagine Effie, if she were present, liking this lyric. It is greeted by "Hmh." Erato, muse of love poetry, prefers the first, Melpomene, muse of tragedy, the second, and Urania, muse of astronomy and heavenly inspiration, the third. Scrutumnus, who judged these poems shortly before his death, liked only the first one. His adverse judgments on the other two, along with the comments and actions of the disciples, are a neat satirical summary of Leavisite criticism, a very "low mimetic" creed.[8]

The first principle, the great value of evaluating literature, is a perversion of Arnold's touchstone method. Other criteria follow: good taste, expression of real emotion, language of the people, simplicity of diction, no obscurity. These lead to a condemnation of high-sounding themes and images and, finally, of the muse of lyric poetry herself. We notice in passing that Scrutumnus is much more articulate as to why he dislikes a poem than he is in giving sound reasons for his preference. The tendency in some quarters for Leavisites to accuse those who disagree with their canon of being sexually perverted gets a wallop, in Lobo's question about Terpsichore, "Who's this skirted lesbian stench?" The names of the disciples who put the critic ahead of literature itself (Terpsichore is told she must bow to the critic, "for he's the norm") suggest their functions vis-à-vis literature. "Lobo" indicates someone whose brain has been partly removed through a lobotomy. "Blot" is the one who likes the idea of critically blotting out much of what has formerly been thought good. "Busto" likes poets who "mean exactly what they state" and tries to "bust" Terpsichore, calling her 'Nymph of Sciolism" (pretentious superficiality of knowledge). The Leavisite comments on *Finnegans Wake* and *The Tyger* suggest that for all his prizing of erotic literature the great critic is basically a kind of Anti-creativity figure, rather like Antichrist.

The Eclogue's main satirical points, then, are two. When literary criticism proceeds on too narrow a base, it ends up dis-

posing of most of the world's great literature. And secondly, all
critical value judgments, however valid and acceptable they
are for those who share the critic's tastes and prejudices, are in-
demonstrable. Hence the large amount of invective in Leavisite
controversies and the tendency to "storm" when to prove the
evaluative point is clearly impossible.

XII   *The September Eclogue*

As early as "The March Eclogue" the reader's attention has
been pointed forward to "September," for what Effie (who understands more of the purgatorial process through which the
geese are being put than any of the others do) calls "a general
nostalgie de la boue." The Classicist Mopsus, who has considerable intellectual curiosity, has suggested that he and Branwell
take the sibylline Effie along to Mome Fair to explain things
there. All this was said at the end of an eclogue which set up
two antithetical visions, one of a malign, lunar world of nothingness, the other of a green and gold paradisal one; in between
was the area in which Effie turned the goose eggs and instructed
her friends, and where the Doorknob showed the farmhouse
children "How to be Ham, Japhet and Shem / And drunken
Noah." These three geese, also Dorcas and George, find at
Mome Faire in "September" what Yeats would call their "fated
images."

"Mome" is a Spenserian word for "bumpkin." It is also an
anglicization of the Greek *Momus,* the personification or god
of ridicule, used with an extended meaning in English as "a
fault-finder." Sir Philip Sidney, in the last paragraph of his
Apologie for Poetrie, speaks contemptuously of people of an
"earth-creeping" mind which "cannot lift itself up to look to the
sky of poetry" because of "a certain rustical disdain." This kind
of mind, he says, "will become such a mome as to be a Momus
of poetry." Lewis Carroll used Mome to mean "away from
home."

All these meanings are relevant. In "September" the bump-
kins or rustic geese leave home and go to town to stare at the
sights of a fall fair. The satirical *mythos* of the whole poem
comes to a climax here, in what Reaney clearly intends as a huge
Joycean anti-epiphany suggesting the whole of Western culture,

including Canadian history, revolving against a background of loud screams from a newly-born baby, the playing of a blind fiddler, and a drunken preacher's sermon about Judas and all other degenerates who help the Holy Ghost in the betrayal of Jesus. There is an exhibit of prize animals and plants who are human character-types and a funhouse of Canadian history which is also Dante's Inferno. Branwell, so the Argument of the Eclogue tells us, "went into the funhouse again & again for another look at the horse-eating iris." The merry-go-round is an imagistic account of Western thought from the Eleatics to the Existentialists. Mopsus particularly likes this. The ferris wheel, favored by Dorcas and George, is organized round images of comparative religion and fertility rituals culled from Sir James Frazer's *Golden Bough*. A caterpillar ride suggestively but briefly illustrates the rapidity with which an individual human life passes, and a sideshow of miscreated things holds the imperturbable Effie's gaze.

On the whole the prize animals and plants appear to be broadly descriptive of certain human character-types, symbolic rather than explicitly allegorical. One of them, however, refers to a specific figure from Canadian history; the others give the impression of being based in enigmatic ways on actual persons known to Reaney, and one of them is, although to identify him would be libelous. In his notes to the reader at the beginning of the book, Reaney indicates the historical figure behind his Pouter Pigeon. This is the infamous (from the poet's point of view) Bishop Bourget of nineteenth century French-Canadian history who did a great deal to keep British and European liberalism out of French Canada when they belatedly began to appear in such forms as the anti-clerical *Institut Canadien*, the only significant opposition to Conservatism in Lower Canada. As Donald Creighton points out in *Dominion of the North*,[9] the Roman Catholic Church in French Canada had an old tradition of illiberality and Ultramontanism which was considerably fortified by the publication of Pope Pius IX's *Syllabus of Errors* in 1846 and by the declaration of papal infallibility in 1870. The *Institut Canadien* had come out in support of non-sectarian state education, had criticized religious orders, had admitted to its membership both Protestant and English Canadians, and had included in its library a few Protestant and skeptical volumes—all of which brought on it the wrath of Bourget and, ultimately, of Rome. In 1869 the Montreal hierarchy succeeded in having members of the *Institut* forbidden the sacraments. It is at this point that Reaney's portrait of the Pouter Pigeon comes into focus.

Pouter pigeons are noted, of course, for their great power of inflating their crops. Reaney's, with "Crozier, cap and scarlet carillon," stands pouting at a window and calling out to a hearse which rolls up, "Stone it shakers! Stone it my doves!" Those in charge of the hearse succeed in burying their "poor heretic," however, and in coating his coffin with concrete, lest "Pouter Pigeon may perhaps pry him up." Not to be frustrated, Bishop Pouter has all the other inmates of the cemetery, "the faithful finikins," moved to another site.

(The historical facts underlying this vignette are as follows. In 1869, the year in which Bishop Bourget succeeded in having the members of the *Institut* barred from the sacraments, one of them, a devout Roman Catholic called Joseph Guibord, died suddenly without the last rites of the church and was accordingly denied burial in sanctified ground. The *Institut* fought the issue from one court to another and finally received a favorable decision from the Judicial Committee of the Privy Council, the supreme civil authority. When Guibord's body was taken from its temporary resting place in a Protestant vault for burial in a Roman Catholic cemetery, it was stoned and driven away by the enraged "faithful." Finally, on a rainy November day six years after Guibord's death, he was buried in the Côte des Neiges cemetery, his coffin encased in cement and scrap-metal to protect if from the Roman Catholic laity. The Roman clergy, though, were not to be outdone. Bishop Bourget deconsecrated the place in which Guibord was buried.)

Other exhibits include the following: a perambulating, sleek Tom Cat; a prize dog, an obscene militaristic figure; a pig, a figure of the most rudimentary mental development and of swinish sensuality; a hen called "Hohum humble" who "hiked herself to Sunday School" but never nudged her neck up to the sky; a "Fanciful flighty fairy cow" full of exuberant energy and the capacity for excessive physical pleasures; a closed gentian, a thing of contradictions and treacherous beauty, an aristocratic image of privileged social caste, a Family Compact sort of figure.

The Canadianism and the enigmatic style of *A Suit of Nettles* come to their climax in the next passage, entitled "Dante's Inferno & Funhouse." We are told that this is "an attempt to compress Canadian history and geography into a single horrific scenic railway ride" and that the facts can be found in Creighton's *Dominion of the North*. Now something of a classic statement of Canadian history, Creighton's book is a chronological account extending from 1500 to the 1950's. It would be impossible to make much sense of this part of Reaney's poem without a knowledge of Canadian history; this is entirely deliberate, one manifestation of many in Reaney's writings of his impatience with Canadians who are so intent on learning about Europe or the United States that they remain permanently ignorant about their own environment. If the reader is not actively interested in Canada, historically and geographically, he cannot proceed very far with one major part of the poem's symbolism. Even with a knowledge of Creighton's text and the requisite interest, Reaney's funhouse does not readily yield up all its secrets.

The seventeen italicized entries which make up the places, things, persons, and dates of the train ride of Canadian history are accompanied by emblematic images designed to show the infernal character of that history. The references range from the immediately obvious to the very obscure. First, beginning in the east of Canada, we have *Rivière du Loup,* suggesting a wolf-infested wilderness world, with the emblem "A huge gasping gaping jaw narrowing to rapids." Northrop Frye has commented that entry into Canada from the east via the St. Lawrence River is like entry into a very large whale. Also working here, as part of the Dantesque design, is the medieval Physiologus icon of the gaping mouth of the whale as the gate of hell. *Castor grassus,* "A small room padded with beaver fur," indicates the primacy of the fur trade in early Canadian history; it is one of the rooms of hell in Reaney's poem because in his reading of Canadian history, as can also be seen by Dorcas' account in "February," the spoliation of natural resources has loomed disproportionately large compared to the development of the country's intellectual resources.

[84]

This Tottery Dance

Montreal and *Niagara Falls* together have a place in hell, "A room painted with demon faces, arms holding out white dogs, drums beating, rushing roaring sound." The quality of nightmare apparitions suddenly looming up in the style of *objets trouvés* art to startle and shock the seeing eye is not unlike Dante's handling of the various sights encountered by Virgil and himself; where Reaney is cryptically imagistic, however, the medieval allegorist provides more in the way of explicit commentary on the significance of his numerous figures. Montreal and Niagara are joined in one entry, possibly because of the closeness of the historical development of Lower and Upper Canada and because of the way they both tend to beat the drums of their respective French and English causes while moving towards their "rushing roaring" descent further into the whirlpool circles of their history. In this complex of associations, it seems, we have a symbol of the central spiritual and cultural dichotomy of Canadian historical existence.

The next entry, *Louis XV*, "A shower of milk and a swarm of honey bees," is associated by the poet in a footnote with the use of milk and honey in French coronation rites. Reaney includes the reference to Louis XV for the obvious reason that it was during his reign, in 1759, that Quebec fell to James Wolfe's army, and French rule in northern North America came to an end. Probably more important, though, for the subsequent story of Canada, is the fact that although French Canada was militarily defeated on the Plains of Abraham, the culture of Louis XV was still very much alive. And as Creighton points out, as one of his major themes in *Dominion of the North*, it was the pre-revolutionary culture of France which continued in Quebec, relatively untouched by the so-called Age of Enlightenment until fairly recently. It is in this context that Reaney's references to the reactionary character of Bourget are to be seen.

The entry for *Moraviantown* concerns the period of the War of 1812 in which British North America successfully asserted its will to survive as a separate political entity in the face of United States efforts to impose a political unity on the continent. This part of Reaney's riddling history reads "Freezing cold passage way, lamprey eels pursued by Latvians; an old Indian's skin is turned into horsewhips and shoelaces, deafening explosion."

[85]

Moraviantown in the Talbot Settlement north of Lake Erie was the site of the first U. S. triumph on land over the British forces in 1813, following the naval victory by Perry at Put-in-Bay which had given the U. S. forces control of Lake Erie. These American successes, however, had little more than local significance. Supplies and reinforcements for British posts at Michilimackinac and further west were rerouted by Lake Simcoe and Georgian Bay, for the "Freezing cold passage way" to the northwest, while British and American boats, in Creighton's words (p. 199), "chased and banged each other around the lake." Lake Erie for many years has been infested by the lamprey eel, the pseudo-fish with sucker mouth and eel shape which has done much to ruin the fishing in the Lake. It is a good demonic image for one of the infernal places of Canadian geography and possibly, more specifically, from a Canadian nationalist poet's point of view, for the constant threat of American domination of Canadian life, which reached one of its peaks in the War of 1812. The old Indian's skin which is turned into horsewhips and shoelaces seems to have both a general and a specific reference to the generally inhumane treatment of the Canadian Indian by the British, compared with the French, and to the death of the Shawnee chief Tecumseh, whose skin became a utilitarian object of barter for the Americans.

With the next entry we arrive, chronologically, at the period of the rebellions of 1837 in Upper and Lower Canada: *Mackenzie* "A bloody divan wearing a lace fichu awaits you in this room." William Lyon Mackenzie was the main theorist of political and social revolution and the leader of the rebellion against what he and others thought of as the irresponsible oligarchy of the Family Compact group in Upper Canada, with its loyalty to the Church of England, its control of the state, its efforts to control education, and its Clergy Reserves. As Dorcas summed it up in "February," "The first son played cards, went to properchurch; / The second son did plot beneath a beer vat much." Mackenzie's attempt at reform in Upper Canada, by using the American republican method of popular election, came to a head in the Declaration of the Toronto Reformers adopted on July 31 at Doel's Brewery, followed by the abortive and unsuccessful rising at Montgomery's Tavern north of Toronto on December 4. The image of the bloody divan wearing a lace fichu as it awaits its visitor in Reaney's hell is an allusion to Mackenzie's comment about "Victoria on her bloody divan."

The next room of the Inferno is associated with three places in Saskatchewan, the two Métis communities of *Dawson Road* and *Batoche* and the city of *Regina*. These bring us in time to the period 1870-1885 in which the semi-nomadic culture of the Métis in the valley of the Saskatchewan River—half-French and half-Indian and traditionally involved in hunting the buffalo and in carrying furs and supplies for the Hudson's Bay Company—was disrupted by the coming to the West of the Canadian Pacific Railway and large numbers of settlers of diverse cultural origins. The poet writes, "Go fast through this steam chamber where a Red Nose glowing confronts an Eye glaring. A White Horse is also having quite a time with a monster horse-eating iris which has NEVER FORGET printed on its petals. A pouter pigeon struts by." A footnote explains the "Red Nose glowing" as a reference to the Conservative Prime Minister Sir John A. Macdonald, whose nose, if we are to believe the legend, glowed with political acumen as well as alcoholic stimulus. Creighton describes it this way: "His nose, that large, sensitive, and unerring organ" (p. 330). Another footnote explains "an Eye glaring" as Louis Riel.

The room is a steam chamber, presumably because it was the steam-propelled locomotives of the new transcontinental railway which were the visible sign of the federally supported settlement of the West, which in turn was the major cause of dissension between residents of Manitoba and Saskatchewan, on the one hand, and Macdonald and the federal government, on the other. After Louis Riel in 1869 led his unsuccessful rebellion at Red River against union with Canada, the Métis migrated further west, to take up free land as squatter farmers in the Saskatchewan valley. Here once again, in 1884, Riel became their leader and, backed by many Indians, led the opposition against the federal power. By 1885, when Riel mustered a group of Métis against a detachment of the Mounted Police, he had forfeited his earlier support from French-speaking clergy and English-speaking half-breeds. When 8,000 troops attacked Riel's force at Batoche, he was defeated and the Indian resistance crumbled.

Riel was subsequently tried, found guilty, and hanged at Regina.

Reaney's fascination with Riel is part of his general liking for the rebels of Canadian history who represent forces of life breaking through repressive barriers; it is also justified in terms of the Métis leader's importance in Canadian history. As Creighton points out (p. 364), the agitation over Riel's fate threw into relief all the principal contrasts which distinguished Canada's two main ethnic groups and began a political revolution which basically changed the balance of Canadian public life. The reactionary and illiberal Quebec church, always fiercely conservative in politics, saw its grip on politics loosened shortly after Riel's death, when outraged French-Canadian nationalism found a more suitable champion in the new provincial premier, the Liberal Honoré Mercier. A little later, on the federal level, the Conservatives began to lose Quebec support and in 1896 were completely defeated.

There is more, however, than "historical allegory" working here. At the time Reaney was composing A *Suit of Nettles* he published an article on E. J. Pratt's poetic handling of the building of the first transcontinental railway in Canada in the epic *Towards the Last Spike*. In addition to demonstrating Reaney's grasp of Pratt's purpose, this article can serve as a prose analogue to his own compression of Canadian history and geography "into a single horrific scenic railway ride."[10] Reaney points out that *Towards the Last Spike* is not at all the usual poem about the usual pioneer struggle in Canada, but rather the account of a struggle against Nature which is a struggle against something inside the human mind as well. Principal figures like Sir John A. Macdonald and Van Horne fight against their inability to express to others their vision of Canada as a unified and civilized country rather than as just a vast wilderness of rock, muskeg, and prairie. Here, in the area of mental heroism, they emerge as part of a reality deeper than that which concerns the historian, a reality to which the poet must penetrate if he is not simply to write pseudo-history:

. . . a poet is allowed a view of another reality deep at the source of human consciousness where primeval Canada, primeval Europe, the primeval world are one and the same interesting monster who through the course of time assumes so many different masks. At this

[88]

source, Sir John A. Macdonald, Elizabeth I whom he is rather like with Louis Riel as his Mary Stuart, Andrew Jackson, the questing knights of King Arthur's Court are one and the same opponent of this monster. (p. 20)

This both explains why Reaney finds Macdonald and Riel key figures and brings us to the image of the White Horse "having quite a time" with the monster horse-eating iris to which Branwell, the protagonist of the poem, is so fatally attracted. Even without the aid of the article on Pratt's poem, one could surmise that the White Horse pitted against the monster trying to destroy it has a mythical, heroic resonance. Also, in the context of *A Suit of Nettles*, we have previously met the monstrous rat and the hooting owl which threaten to destroy Branwell's mental powers. So far as Branwell is concerned, it is a matter of the still unresolved conflict in his psyche which draws him to the symbolic opposites of White Horse and monster iris. Until this point, the defection of Dorcas has unleashed forces inside him that he has not known how to handle and which have therefore nearly plunged him into a death of the soul. The White Horse provides, whether Branwell can assimilate its meaning or not, the antithetical image with which to combat the monstrous forces in the human psyche which can be forgotten only with peril. So far as Canadian history is concerned, the Mackenzies and the Macdonalds, all together, are the questing knight or heroic form which fights the primordial monster in the Canadian mind which, if unbeaten, will leave the geographic vastness which Canada is, before the human imagination takes hold of it, an untamed wilderness. The pouter pigeon strutting by represents the Bourgets, the authoritarians and reactionaries who resist those daring to break new ground either in the human mind or in social reconstruction.

The next room of the infernal funhouse is associated with *Craigellachie*, the place in Eagle Pass in the heart of the Rocky Mountains where the last spike of the Canadian Pacific Railway was driven on November 7, 1885. George Stephen and Donald Smith, two of the Scots who built the railway, knew a rock in Scotland called Craigellachie, the meeting place of the clan Grant where a fiery cross had been seen calling the clansmen to battle (Creighton, p. 351). At one point in 1884, when the vast railway enterprise was threatened with financial disaster, Stephen secured an advance in London and cabled Smith in Montreal, "Stand fast, Craigellachie." This room of hell, in Reaney's words, "seems like a railway carriage running on a monorail attached to the crotches of a row of bearded gentlemen all standing in a row with tophats on." Metaphorically, the railroad is a long penis-like single steel line stretched across the country by the indomitable Scots-Canadians—Stephen, Duncan McIntyre, Richard B. Angus, Smith, and, behind these, Sir John A.—the heroes from top-hatted Victorian times who conquered Pratt's "folded reptile," the Pre-Cambrian shield.

The next entry is for *Laurier:* "You are smoking a pipe; the conductor says, 'Défense de fumer.'" Three ideas appear to be working here. "Défense de fumer" is of course a notice seen in Canadian trains, in one of which we are supposed to be riding. Reaney uses the French language sign for the obvious reason that Wilfrid Laurier was the first Canadian Prime Minister of French descent. The third allusion involved is to Laurier's combination of instinctive graciousness and fastidious aloofness. Creighton recounts the impact of Laurier on those around when he first appeared, elegantly dressed, with gloves, stick, and silk hat, for his swearing-in ceremony as Prime Minister (pp. 383-4).

The political battle which raged in 1911 over reciprocal trade with the United States, and which led to the downfall of the dominantly pro-reciprocity Liberal government under Laurier, gets its emblem in the poem from a favorite Conservative opposition poster of the period; its symbolism is clear, in terms of the Canadian nationalist sentiment and the fears of too intimate economic connections with the United States which prevailed at the time: "A Tiger yowls by with a lady on his back." R. L. Borden, who was to be the next Prime Minister, summed up for many Canadians their inveterate hatred of North American continentalism and American talk of "Manifest Destiny," when he told them on the eve of the election that they must decide whether Canadianism or Continentalism was to prevail on the northern half of the continent. Creighton helps to explain Reaney's use of the American tiger in his Canadian hell:

The great majority of the Canadians who voted in the election of 1911 had watched the American intervention in the Venezuelan

boundary dispute, the founding of the American Empire in the Carib-
bean and the Pacific, the American participation in the politics of
the Colombian Republic, and, above all, the American diplomatic
victory in the Alaskan boundary dispute. From this record of the
past, the Canadians drew the conclusion that an active policy of
American imperialism was at work. . . ." (p. 434)

Although fifty-five years later the details now differ slightly, the
symbol chosen by Borden's supporters and used by Reaney still
has its informing power for many Canadians.

At this point (from 1912 onwards) in the fictional train ride,
the grimness of Reaney's use of the word "Funhouse" becomes
unmistakable, as the Canadian train of state encounters really
serious trouble. First there is the disastrous sinking of the
"Titanic" ("The train comes to grief in a drift of flourdough").
In his article on Pratt Reaney mentions how the "Titanic," long
before it hit the iceberg, had hit "another sort of iceberg, a
mental one, that of proud, complacent stupidity that cancels
out the civilization the ship carries" (p. 19). Then comes
World War I, followed by the depression and World War II.
For the first war, we reader-wanderers through Reaney's hell
stumble into a room where a man is being "trepanned" and "a
lineup of 100,000 are all waiting to be in deathly silence." The
reference to trepanning or boring human skulls (this was
practiced by certain Indian tribes) suggests the mass superstition or widespread failure to use its thinking powers which
characterizes a society in a state of war. The "pale beaver" who
accompanies the reader and everyone else in the room, and who
instructs us "to duck ghost cobwebs," is Mackenzie King.

But the corruption of Canadian life in the twentieth century
is internal as well as European in its source. In 1937, after the
depression has ravaged the country for eight years, the federal
government is still showing itself unable to act in any decisive
way. As Reaney puts it, "A horrible smell fills the room: every
time the attendants try to turn on ventilating fans a group of
stately voices say, 'No. You are interfering with the right to
smell.'" Reaney's humanitarian and socialist sympathy is clearly
with the 500,000 unemployed Canadians left to their own devices, so far as the federal power was concerned, when Prime
Minister Bennett's very belated attempts to remedy the situation
foundered in misunderstanding and opposition. The climax

came after the Conservative defeat in 1935. In 1937, as Reaney points out in a note quoting Creighton, "The Judicial Committee of the Privy Council judicially condemned virtually any national plan to cope with any Canadian depression." In Reaney's words, "Bennett's New Deal interfered with the right of the provinces to be depressed."

The "solution" to Canada's depression problems came with World War II in 1939, but at a terrible cost. The last room in the Funhouse is "lined with freshly bleeding scalps" and connects with "A small spiral tunnel, rather messy" which "leads you to a beach where sea serpents and glass bubbles float towards you"; this apparently is a reference to the fateful Dieppe raid of August 19, 1942, in which almost 3,000 Canadians either died, were fatally wounded, or were taken prisoner. Dieppe remains in the Canadian consciousness as one of the bleakest symbols of the ravages of the War. The sea serpents remind us that in one part of Reaney's metaphorical pattern our journey through the hell of Canadian history has been a descent into a demonic whale. The apocalypse described by the funhouse has begun with a wolf image and now, at the conclusion, makes use of serpents. Since a Scandinavian reference is working in the next few lines, it may be relevant to recall that in the apocalypse described by the Sibyl in the "Voluspa" the primordial wolf and serpent are represented as breaking loose. The floating glass bubbles (mines?) are of human manufacture, like much else in Canada's hell.

Reaney's style is enigmatic to the very end. *Port Moody*, on the west coast of Canada, indicates that the trip—past demon faces, human spectres, malign beasts, and monsters to assault the sight, rushing roaring sounds to strike the ear, and a horrible stench to offend the nose—this trip has ended in its geographic destination. But as we emerge into the fair again, we find ourselves "stepping over a dead warrior with flaxen hair who must have tried to get in the wrong way." Creighton's history begins with a one-paragraph account of the little that is known of the first European visitors to North America, the Norsemen, who apparently in the year 1000 discovered the continent and got at least as far south as the Gulf of St. Lawrence in their exploration of what much later became Canada. The Norsemen may even, although this has yet to be proved or disproved, have penetrated the continent by way of Hudson Bay. So far as is known, they did not really get into the intractable, monstrous physical fact which geographical Canada is. It is apparently in this context of an abortive Viking attempt to enter Canada, some five hundred years before Cabot and Cartier, that we are meant to see the image of the dead warrior with flaxen hair. For almost a thousand years warriors have battled with the monster Canada and died. The battle, moreover, is barely begun, Reaney's poem seems to say, at least on the level of finding a symbolic language adequate for a genuine civilization.

The "exhausted old harridan in a cage who is trying to sell tickets" to the funhouse, seen as we emerge, may be connected with the "leather skinned harridan" Granny Crack, who speaks from an ancestral Canadian past and keeps watch over at least some of Canada's mysteries in *Twelve Letters to a Small Town* and *One-man Masque*.

The merry-go-round which follows the funhouse is a burlesque on the theme of remembering key concepts in the history of Western philosophy. Here the deadly accuracy of the god of ridicule is at work in a delightful way. The prose style imitates the huckstering of a midway barker; those addressed are called "loafkneaders and genitalmen," suggesting that although the sub-ject is philosophy the treatment will be down-to-earth and easily grasped by materialists and sensualists alike. And it is. The method involves the selection of one or more central ideas of fourteen major thinkers (seven classical Greek, three medieval, four modern) and the describing of a horse whose appearance in each case points to the underlying concepts.

First we have *Parmenides*, "a really stock still stoneheavy big Percheron that does not go up and down like the others because as a matter of fact he doesn't believe in it." Parmenides, the classical exponent of a "block-reality" or extreme monism, is singled out for his idea that all change is an illusion of the senses, the true reality being a unity, unchangeable and immov-able and conceivable only by logical thought. The horse *Heracli-tus* is in sharp contrast: "a fiery steed! it goes up and down like nothing but and its whole form keeps flowy-changing; as a matter of fact you can't seem to sit in the same saddle twice on it it seems." According to Heraclitus, there was no permanent reality except the reality of change; permanence was an illusion of the senses. Therefore the only possible real state was the transitional one of becoming: "All things flow; we cannot step twice into the same river." He believed fire to be the underlying substance of the universe and all other elements to be transformations of it.

Plato's universe (he follows Heraclitus on the merry-go-round) accommodates the changeless being of Parmenides and the constant flux of Heraclitus. Plato argued for the independent reality of Ideas as the only sure basis of objective scientific knowledge. These Ideas, eternal, changeless, and indefinite in number, are the Forms or Archetypes of all concrete things. He explained the physical world as possessing only relative reality, by virtue of its participation in the reality of the Ideas. In the *Phaedrus* we have the clearest discussion of mystical contemplation of the Idea. It is the world of Ideas which gives life and significance to the world of the senses. The most famous explanation of this is the parable of the cave in the *Republic*. These ideas Reaney captures in one ludicrously apt figure: "here's a beautiful white horse—peculiar—it's a beeyootiful glass horse sailing above it and the horse you're sitting on keeps looking up in the most sort of ridiculous way trying to do exactly what the glass horse is doing but of course it just looks like a cheap imitation particularly since it keeps looking up all the time and the beautiful glass horse has such poise it never looks anywhere except straight ahead."

It is not *Aristotle* the metaphysician, the biologist, the astronomer, or the psychologist who takes the form of "a rather stocky Clydesdale with three saddles, three heads and three buttocks." This is the author of the *Nichomachean Ethics* who celebrated the Greek notion of the golden mean, or nothing in excess: "one buttock is too hairy, the middle one is just right and the left hand one has no hair at all."

Democritus, who lived before Aristotle, comes "just behind him," although all the other horses of the merry-go-round appear chronologically. Perhaps there is here an unstated but deliberate connection with twentieth-century atomic theory and the Einsteinian relativity hypothesis. In any case, the immediate impact of this horse has a clear conceptual base in the Democritean atomic theory, by which a postulated constant motion of atoms helps to explain the creation of worlds. For Democritus the heavier atoms form the earth, the lighter ones the heavenly bodies. So far as man's cognition is concerned, sense perception yields only confused knowledge; thought alone can apprehend the nature of things. So Reaney's Democritus is "a very shifty galloway—all sand as a matter of fact, all whirling around and you're in danger of sinking into your saddle up to your topknot."

For *Epicurus* Reaney's image and implicit comment point to the centuries-old popular misconception of Epicurus and his teaching. The "drunken old nag with a wreath of poppies slung about its neck" is the stock figure of self-indulgent forgetfulness, not the man who taught that *ataraxia* or serenity and intellectual pleasure are far superior to bodily pleasures. There may also be working obliquely in Reaney's image, however, the historically accurate view of Epicurus' emancipation from all superstitious fears of death and future punishment, through the adoption of a Democritean atomism freed of some of its deterministic implications and thus permitting a doctrine of free will.

Reaney's *Zeno* is Zeno of Citium, the founder of Stoicism, not Zeno of Elea. He is a "sorry nag with its bottom up in the air because it's subduing its bottom and that's the surest way of tiring your bottom out. Its skin is all leathery; it leathers it by beating it against the walls of its stall so that if anyone *should* beat it, you see, why it wouldn't feel this at all." This parodies the Stoic view that harmony with nature and oneself is the ideal life, that the most important thing for an individual to learn is self-sufficiency, through a rigorous training of the will, and a sense of duty based on strong belief in the overruling power of divine providence.

St. Augustine is more complicated, a horse whose "rear quarters are half pitch dark and half blinding white and no amount of dye will ever get the beast either one colour or the other." A Manichean and dualist for nine years before his conversion to Christianity, Augustine displays in his writings a profound sense of his own concupiscence and, like Calvin later, teaches that but for the grace of God man can do no good thing. Hence Reaney notes, "There's a certain marionette like quality about this horse's prancing as if every capriole were destined by some other force than the horse's mind." One last satirical gibe is leveled at Augustine's tendency almost to exult in how evil he is: "This horse wears a certain self-satisfied look on his face as if he knew a secret nightmare no one else did."

Aquinas, who in his time was nicknamed the Dumb Ox, because of his slowness of manner and his stoutness, emerges in *A Suit of Nettles* as "a very fat round mare" which "slops by looking as if she bore twin foals." These offspring, predictably, are Aristotle's philosophy ("a classic stallion") and Christian revelation ("a milkwhite unicorn filly"), both "unified within her." The Thomist mare is dismissed with the comment, "Well, let her amble by." This suggests two things in the satirist's view of Thomism. First there is the achievement of teaching a horse something as unnatural as "ambling," moving forward by lifting the two feet on one side together, rather than by alternating them. This does make for a very comfortable ride, however artificial the accomplishment. And secondly, it suggests the sense that for Reaney the relevance of Thomism has receded into history.

Closely and unerringly, so far as images are concerned, *Duns Scotus* is correlated with Aquinas. He is presented as the founder of the school of Scholasticism opposed to the Thomism of Aquinas' followers; "a lean pale horse," he trots behind the mare, smirking at her girth and completeness. Duns Scotus taught that certain knowledge of the existence of God, of the immortality of the soul, and of resurrection is not possible through scientific means; also that the objects of faith are never logically necessary. His skepticism and his emphasis on the relative character of religious knowledge give him a place as a pioneer of nominalism, a manner of thinking appropriate to materialist and empirical philosophy; hence his "knowing look as if let's not talk about a full manger laid up in heaven when work is over but let's have a look at just a wisp of hay here right in front of me."

The "pretty snow white horse" symbolizing Jakob *Boehme* (1575-1624), a German Anabaptist visionary with a considerable influence on one of Reaney's poetic mentors, William Blake, brings us to the one thinker of the merry-go-round who would not normally be included in a survey of Western philosophy; significantly, Boehme is the one figure of the fourteen who receives no ridiculing comment. In a burst of apocalyptic imagery similar to that found in Boehme's visionary writings themselves, we are shown his central doctrine of the play of contraries within the will at the heart of all creation. The text alluded to here seems to be the early work *Aurora*, in which Boehme proclaims God as the origin of all creation, in every aspect of which he is revealed. God in himself contains all antithetical principles. At one time he is love and light; Reaney puts it this way, "tattooed with stars, mountains meadows real sheep moving on them it seems & fiery comets & ships in a harbour & little horses dancing in a barnyard. This horse's eyes—oh the angelic aurora wonder of its gold red mane." Again he is fire and wrath: "Storms break out in the tattooed skies and a fiery fire burns in the eyes." But God as wrath torments himself inwardly until he again releases love: "it bubbles over—a light comes into his eyes and the world changes back again."

This Blakean exuberance contrasts with the mechanistic precision of *Descartes*, "a smart little fossil horse large as a fox ticking as if it worked mechanically with melted beeswax in its feedbag and a distinctly mathematical looking hoof." It was with the aim of extending mathematical method to all areas of human knowledge that Descartes developed his methodology. Discarding the authoritarian system of the Scholastics, he began with universal doubt, proceeded through his famous *Cogito, ergo sum* to the existence of God, and thence to the reality of the physical world; God would not deceive the thinking mind by perceptions that are illusions, and therefore the external world we perceive must exist. Reaney's Cartesian horse, suitably then, shows "a tendency to go for weighty things like lumps of coal you may hand him" but, as a good rationalist, "doesn't go for painted butterflies or candy sugar sticks." It is followed by the "brutish nasty and short small fat merrylegs of a pit pony speckled all over with the pitchings of flies" which represents the most famous of the ideas of Thomas *Hobbes*. In the *Leviathan* (1651) Hobbes argued mechanistically that man naturally is a selfishly individualistic animal constantly at war with all other men. In the state of nature, before any political organization develops, men are equal one with another in their self-seeking and exist in a life which is "nasty, brutish, and short."

Heidegger, the last horse of the merry-go-round, both continues the historical line from those preceding him (Hobbes has his teeth in Heidegger's hind quarters) and brings the pattern full circle ("I believe it's the horse we started out with, only, since we saw it last it may have changed a bit"). Three aspects of Heidegger's thought emerge through the images. From Kierkegaard, Heidegger took as his problem the tragic nature of being in a finite world and the sense of anguish and forlornness which bears down on man as he comes to know the unavoidable limits of his life. From Husserl and the phenomenologists, Heidegger borrowed introspection and subjective analysis as valid tools for the study of human nature and, in so doing, dispensed with the restraints and consolations of traditional philosophical and religious method. The anguish and the subjectivism in Heidegger lead Reaney to the fantasy of a horse which is "a foundered staggered old thing—covered with boils, rather agonized and heavy looking." Heidegger believes, moreover, that by comprehending and accepting the limitations of existence man can, by "resolute decision," transcend the everyday world and assert his essence. And so we have Reaney's horse "looking as if it might leap for the sky." The connection with *Parmenides*, the first horse, would seem to lie in the common emphasis on the necessity to transcend through thought the illusory, unsatisfactory world of the senses.

Reaney's placing of philosophical concepts and theories into the context of a rural Ontario fair provides a kind of quixotic satire rare in Canadian literature. His reduction of major philosophical systems to "an endless string of gracefully up and downing wooden horses all pursuing a brass ring labelled TRUTH" (in several instances the reference is only to the back end of a horse) is of course not to be taken as flagrant anti-intellectualism on the poet's part, or even as his reasoned view of philosophy as a discipline. Like William Blake in his attitude to the relations between thinkers read by him, Reaney could say here, "I will not Reason & Compare."

What he is doing, primarily, is continuing a well-established traditional satire on the abstracting, over-simplifying tendencies of much philosophical speculation, the kind of thing Butler decries in his satire on the "Colleges of Unreason." This is partly a matter of poetry's defense against what to the imagistic poet like Reaney must seem the comparatively naive and highly repetitive nature of philosophy over the centuries. By reducing a philosophy to a simple image or two, he at once points to the core of its significance and to what in his view is its absurdly abtstract aspect. The different attitude shown towards Boehme is Reaney's way of saying that when philosophy leaves out fiery, poetic vision and the question of redemptive power, it ceases to be useful. The sterile landscape of the human minds exposed in *A Suit of Nettles* needs more than a beautiful Platonic glass horse sailing above the actual world and never looking anywhere except straight ahead. Speculative detachment has its strong appeal for the philosophical goose Mopsus, at least up to this point in the poem, but it is clear that the "hour-long explorations" of the "life and heart and mind-line" of the inhabitants of the farm must involve something more comprehensive than abstract thought.

In the image of the Ferris wheel which follows the merry-go-round, Reaney provides his reader with what Sir James Frazer might have called a "curious refinement of savage philosophy." Having shown how the absurdities of abstract thought find their place in a country-fair setting, he now turns his attention to what in some ways are the opposite human phenomena, primitive magic and religion and the rites and practices involved in them. The major inspiration here is Frazer's *Golden Bough*, that classic of cultural anthropology which appeared first as two volumes in 1890, then expanded to twelve, then contracted to one very large (756 pages) abridged volume in 1922,[11] and now has been scientifically tidied up as *The New Golden Bough*, edited and annotated by Theodor H. Gaster (1959). It is the third of these which Reaney, like several other important twentieth-century writers, uses, not as an anthropological textbook but as a source of images and literary patterns appropriate to his over-all theme of fertility and sterility, to his seasonal account of life on a farm, and to his fable about a young poet-goose enveloped in green leaves dying a sacrificial death.

The poet tells us that when you are on the Ferris wheel you do not notice the phenomenon under investigation because "by that time you're a clown enjoying your pastime." The perspective we are invited to take, then, is the same one required by all the other enigmas of this intricately worked out poem, that of "learneds" enjoying an intellectual puzzle. Here Reaney borrows the terms Frazer used to distinguish himself, as anthropologist, and other educated Europeans, from the savages he describes in the midst of their primitive actions: at one point Frazer talks of "the quaint rites which in Europe have long dwindled into mere fossils, the pastime of clowns and the puzzle of the learned," as still being living realities in other less developed areas of the globe (p. 413). Reaney's borrowing, however, involves an adaptation of meaning.

The overall satirical stance of the writer is clear in *A Suit of Nettles*. It is evident too in the Ferris wheel section. There are, however, different degrees of sympathy and ridicule established in relation to the various contents of the poem. We have noticed something of this in the handling of the philosophers. Now, although the element of buffoonery is present in the antics described in the seven baskets of the wheel, it is also clear that Reaney's mythopeic imagination finds Frazer's love-hate attitude to the rituals he describes a sympathetic one. Even more important, for anyone trying to penetrate the basic structure and meaning of *A Suit of Nettles*, is the realization of a close similarity between the mythopeic imagination of a twentieth-century poet like Reaney and that of the individuals Frazer calls "savages" (in our generation the word favored is "primitives"). If we make allowances for Frazer's prose rhetoric in the passage cited below, we can see how closely what he says in it about "savage" man's imaginings parallels the mode of imagining illustrated in Reaney's pastoral:

Accustomed to personify the forces of nature, to tinge her cold abstractions with the warm hues of imagination, to clothe her naked realities with the gorgeous drapery of mythic fancy, he fashioned for himself a train of gods and goddesses, of spirits and elves, out of the shifting panorama of the seasons, and followed the annual fluctuations of their fortunes with alternate emotions of cheerfulness and dejection, of gladness and sorrow, which found their natural expression in alternate rites of rejoicing and lamentation, of revelry and mourning (p. 386).

The poet's mythopeia is of course a literary matter, a question of fashioning symbols appropriate to the form and theme of his poem. And this has nothing to do with a latter-day belief in magic or religious superstition, although there seem to be readers and audiences encountering Reaney's works who are incapable of making this basic distinction. One theater-goer disposed of Reaney's play *Listen to the Wind* as "just a fairy tale."

Virtually all the images associated with the seven baskets of the Ferris wheel can be found at least once, and in several cases many times, in the pages of *The Golden Bough*. In the first basket we see a group of "wildly excited louts" chasing a "wild man dressed up in a skin of thick green painted leaves." This image recurs in Frazer and includes the young fellow enveloped in leaves or moss called the Wild Man in the Whitsuntide ceremony in some localities, and known in other places as the Grass King, the King of the May, Jack-in-the-Green, or the Green Wolf, all of whom connect with the Kings of the Wood at Nemi, in accordance with Frazer's large controlling metaphor. The wild man in green also appears as the representative of the spirit of vegetation called Green George. Here, it seems, we learn why Reaney calls one of his principal geese George. The test set for the Green George of folk-ritual was to slip unnoticed out of his leafy envelope at the appropriate moment and substitute an effigy which, instead of him, was thrown into the water at the climax of the fertility ritual. Reaney's George is a virile breeder who succeeds in winning the favors of the poem's prettiest female embodiment of fertility, Dorcas, and who also at the right moment, in December, manages to substitute the scapegoat Branwell for the slaughter.

The second basket involves a set of images which encompass a vast area of meaning in Frazer's book. We see on a miniature scale a bonfire, with men and women dancing round it, changing into a wheel which is then set afire and sent whirling like a huge sunflower down a green mountain. The wheel-flower-dancing people image decreases in size and then, returned to the top of the mountain, becomes large again. Examined closely it still shows "the men and women dancing around like seeds forming in the fire blossoms." From Frazer we learn that the burning wheel represents a variety of things: to it in some places a straw man representing Death was fastened and burned as the wheel rolled down hill, after which Death was replaced by a fir-tree decked in ribbons and clothing (p. 311); along the

Moselle young men guided a blazing wheel down a hill through the vineyards towards the river, in an attempt to get the wheel right into the water before it was stopped by any obstruction, thus ensuring a vintage grape crop (pp. 623-4); in other places the custom of rolling a burning wheel down a hill apparently passed for an imitation of the sun's course in the sky (p. 643). The reader of Frazer will find numerous other ramifications of the fiery wheel as a symbol of primitive attempts to mobilize solar, human, and vegetable energies in the interests of productivity. We remember at this point that one of the female contraception experts in "May" was metamorphosed into an iron maiden used for threshing seeds from ripe sunflowers.

The third basket changes the focus from seedtime to harvest, thus bringing into the poem another complex of meanings to do with the fruits of harvest and those things necessary to be done if a particular harvest is not to be the last one. The image again is that of a circle, this time of reapers in a wheat-field moving towards the last knot of uncut grain at the center. From it a furious bird (or a goose, cat, pig, or little man) hisses up and tries to escape through the reapers' legs. It is caught, killed, and eaten. But the next year it is still there in the last sheaf of grain.

Frazer writes,

> The corn-spirit is supposed to lurk as long as he can in the corn, retreating before the reapers, the binders, and the threshers at their work. But when he is forcibly expelled from his refuge in the last corn cut or the last sheaf bound or the last grain threshed, he necessarily assumes some other form than that of the corn-stalks, which had hitherto been his garment or body (p. 447).

He goes on to list and document these forms and cites all of those used by Reaney. Later he describes how the flesh of the corn-spirit was eaten as a sacrament by his worshippers, part of it being kept till next sowing-time or harvest as a pledge and security that the spirit's energies would not die (p. 470). The use of a human victim is documented from societies remote from Europe (p. 480). Probably the most relevant description in *The Golden Bough* of this kind of ritual, so far as the goose characters of Reaney's poem and their fates are concerned, is the one illustrating the use of a goose as representative of the corn-spirit:

Similarly in Shropshire the name "neck," or "the gander's neck," used to be commonly given to the last handful of ears left standing in the middle of the field when all the rest of the corn was cut. It was plaited together, and the reapers, standing ten or twenty paces off, threw their sickles at it. Whoever cut it through was said to have cut off the gander's neck. The "neck" was taken to the farmer's wife, who was supposed to keep it in the house for good luck till the next harvest came round (p. 446).

The fourth basket continues the ritual progress through the year and is set in "an inverted spring world," November, the rutting season for deer. We are shown antlered "stags leaping up into the air with forests on their heads" and also the same dancers earlier associated with the fiery wheel now leaping over the fire, bringing faggots to it and marching away again, their "eyes of flame polka-dotting the dark forest." The benefits of these rites, Frazer tells us, include early marriage (if one leaps successfully over the fire), plentiful harvest, no backache during the next season's reaping, or a crop as high as the flames leap. The faggots brought to the annual bonfire were carefully preserved from the previous year (p. 630).

Basket Five shows a winter scene in which men and women play cat's cradle as a way of working homeopathic magic for a variety of purposes. Another group dance and beat assorted instruments, including their own heads, apparently in an attempt to banish winter and to keep fire alive: "the snow disappears and out of the ground push the green claws & yellow horns and red tongues of a bonfire." The images here show the close identification of each part of nature with all other parts—the heavenly bodies, men, animals, and fire. The use of the game of cat's cradle takes its suggestion from Frazer but has been extended by Reaney into a generalized symbol of human attempts to manipulate nature:

When the sun is going southward in the autumn, and sinking lower and lower in the Arctic sky, the Esquimaux of Oglulik play the game of cat's cradle in order to catch him in the meshes of the string and so prevent his disappearance. On the contrary, when the sun is moving northward in the spring, they play the game of cup-and-ball to hasten his return (p. 21).

The second-to-last basket shows a happy child, apparently abandoned in a lonely place and surrounded by men in wolf masks. On his head is a green wreath and in his hands a noise-maker and rattle. A mirror, a gift from his stepmother, is wrapped up in front of him. This seems ambiguous enough. Taking the images as they stand, before going outside the context for further help, we have the child who is happy even though surrounded by men in wolf masks, suggesting that the sinister surroundings do not frighten him unduly. This is supported by the fact that he is shaking the noisemaker and rattle. The green wreath would seem, like so much else in this part of the poem, to be a symbol of vegetation and ongoing natural life. Apparently the most menacing detail in the description is the stepmother and her gift of a mirror to the child.

From *The Red Heart* we know that the word "stepmother" is loaded with meaning in Reaney's writings; it connotes all the haunting, malevolent human forces which threaten the happiness and development of the child. Even without reference to Reaney's other works, we might surmise that a stepmother would have this meaning, as it has in dozens of folk-tales and myths— *Snow White and the Seven Dwarfs, Hansel and Gretel,* and *Cinderella* (Reaney reworks the Cinderella story in his play *The Easter Egg),* to name only three of the most familiar. Like the two first of these, *The Seven Swans,* which gives the titular symbol to Reaney's book, concerns children consigned to live in a remote part of nature because of the jealousy of a stepmother. Also, there is a passage in *The Golden Bough* which appears to have provided some of the images and meanings here. In his account of the rites of Dionysus, Frazer tells (p. 388) how the Cretan myth about this particular god involves the jealousy of his stepmother, Queen Juno, and her attempt to dispose of her husband Jupiter's bastard son, fathered on Persephone. Going abroad at one point, Jupiter has turned his throne over to the child Dionysus, who is under the care of supposedly trustworthy guards. Juno, however, bribes these guards and then, by giving the child rattles and a cunningly-wrought looking-glass, lures him into an ambush where the guards surprise and kill him, after which they eat him. Like other vegetation gods, though, Dionysus does not stay dead and his worshippers celebrate his revival. The myth, then, works in the same way as the folk-tales, towards the frustration of the hostile stepmother's plans.

The gift of the mirror would seem to be part of the overall malevolence of the stepmother. Frazer documents the wide-spread belief among primitive peoples that the mirror image or shadow of an individual are his soul or life-spirit (pp. 189-193), to be jealously protected from falling into the clutches of any enemy. The Narcissus-myth, among its many meanings, includes the notion that a narcotic absorption with one's mirror reflection is one sure way never to grow to adulthood. A mirror, then, would seem to be an excellent gift for Juno to give her happy but hated stepson.

One further meaning in this passage may be worth mentioning. At the time *A Suit of Nettles* was taking shape, Reaney, under the influence of Northrop Frye, was reading Carl Jung's psychology of the collective unconscious and of archetypes. Those familiar with Jung's writings may recall his essay on "The Psychology of the Child Archetype"[12] in which he makes certain comments which help explain the contents of this particular basket of the Ferris wheel and perhaps also Reaney's perennial use of the innocent child figure in a hostile environment:

It is a striking paradox in all child myths that the "child" is on the one hand delivered helpless into the power of terrible enemies and in continual danger of extinction, while on the other he possesses power far exceeding those of ordinary humanity. This is closely related to the psychological fact that though the child may be "insignificant," unknown, "a mere child," he is also divine. From the conscious standpoint we seem to be dealing with an insignificant content. . . . Myth, however, emphasizes that it is not so, but that the "child" is endowed with superior powers and, despite all dangers, will unexpectedly pull through. The "child . . . is a personification of vital forces quite outside the limited range of our conscious mind; of ways and possibilities of which our one-sided conscious mind knows nothing; a wholeness which embraces the very depths of Nature. It represents the strongest, the most ineluctable urge in every being, namely the urge to realize itself (p. 170).

The "September Eclogue" begins and ends with references to the wauling infant conceived in "January" up in the peastraw loft by Ann and the hired man Peter. The "Argument" of "September" also tells us that the breeders Dorcas and George, the goose-counterparts of Ann and Peter, particularly like the Ferris wheel. In "May" we have heard how infant geese are threatened both by animals (skunks, turtles, foxes) and by contraception advocates; in spite of such threats to the ongoing life of nature the process continues. It is this fact above all others that the Ferris wheel celebrates, even as it points out the savage limitations of a life lived only in nature.

The last basket contains the Sun and the Moon, described as a benevolent cartoonist might draw them, "with fat round bodies and faces beaming." The Moon, although not so named, is clearly the traditional huntress goddess—she has a dozen or so gray hound-dogs in her arms and lap—and is also the force, along with the Sun, which controls tides, winds, rivers, fountains, and whirlwinds. The Sun and the Moon are married but the Moon is only partly domesticated and is given to wandering, until her husband summons her back. The suggestion here, that only so long as the masculine, solar principle controls the lunar one is there harmony in nature, is not new. When the moon moves too far into a life of her own, as she does in her twenty-eight whorish phases in Branwell's bleak vision of reality in "March," the whole sublunary world is the worse for it. At this point the Sun sends out a falcon to find her. Reaney explores his myth of the Sun and the Moon further in his first comedy, *The Sun and the Moon,* written during the summer of 1958, just after the publication of *A Suit of Nettles.* For the moment we need notice only that in *A Suit of Nettles* life itself is closely identified with the sun, whether in the "dim loose star-knot" of the gosling deep inside the egg, the "golden dart" of spiritual enlightenment entering the human heart, the sunflower wheel of fire, or the sun who takes into his arms the sleeping-beauty earth-goddess in the spring. One of the last images in "September" has to do with the impregnation of the moon by her solar husband: "Sun with its sperm belt spangles against cog moon."

Where the Ferris wheel symbolizes broad, universal patterns in nature in terms of seed-time and harvest, summer and winter, and birth and death, the caterpillar ride focuses very briefly on the youth-age contrast in individual human lives. This ride goes round for a while with its dusky, dusty top down, then opens to show infants "hardening and changing into old men & women." It closes again and repeats the cycle.

The sideshows passage explores another contrast. The Genesis myth of creation is sketched briefly, followed by an account of history in terms of miscreated things, the images of a freak-show. The created universe is old now, its crotch, armpits, and hair full of lice, and it badly needs redemption. Appropriately, then, the first oddity shown us in the sideshows is a huge whale, an image both historical in the narrow sense (the poet knows of such an exhibit throughout Ontario in the 'thirties) and archetypal, having to do with the iconic sea-beast traditionally representative of the temporary conquest of created things by hell. Earlier we saw Canadian history swallowed by such a monster. The freaks are those advertised in any midway series of sideshows, animals and people trained to do unnatural things or born or mutilated into strange shapes. Here too are all the games of chance symbolic of a world fastened resolutely to the wheel of Fortune. The whole sequence is set forth in a quaternity of color—in black, white, yellow, and red tents—and culminates in "the Grotto of the Beautiful Hermaphrodite."

The symbolic Hermaphrodite is crucial to an understanding of "September" and has significance for the whole poem. It is placed at the climactic point in the demonic vision which makes up the bulk of the Eclogue, after the descriptions of the several variants of hell's confining circles and just before the drunken sermon about Christ's passion. Also, coming at the end of the sideshows, it bears comparison with the terminal images of each previous section of the Eclogue: the "star-hell, sterile-pregnant gentian"; the dead warrior with flaxen hair and the old harridan; the agonized old horse Heidegger looking as if it might leap for the sky; the Sun and the Moon; infants and old men. Each of these is an image of opposites, of separation and tension.

Jung tells us[13] that the hermaphrodite means nothing less than a union of the strongest and most striking opposites. It both refers back in time, to a primitive state of mind in which differences and contrasts were either barely separated or completely merged, and also forward, to a goal not yet reached. It is not only a product of primitive non-differentiation but a figure which preoccupies man's imagination even on the highest levels of culture. It has become a "symbol of the creative union of opposites." In spite of its monstrosity and its appropriateness for exhibition in a sleazy midway, the hermaphrodite has traditionally become a subduer of conflicts and a bringer of healing, linked, as Jung notes, with Christ's androgyny in contemporary Catholic mysticism (pointing forward to Reaney's Christ references in the latter part of the poem) and with the *coniugium solis et lunae* in medieval Hermetic philosophy (pointing back to the domesticated Sun and Moon of the Ferris wheel passage). Psychologically the hermaphrodite is a symbol of the unity of personality, of the self when the war of opposites has given way to peace. "In this way," Jung writes, "the primordial being becomes the distant goal of man's self-development, having been from the very beginning a projection of his unconscious wholeness" (p. 175). In his doctoral dissertation on Spenser and Yeats, Reaney describes the hermaphrodite in *The Faerie Queene* as a symbol of "the reflected glory of god in the shape of two lovers embracing" (p. 160).

The Hermaphrodite in *A Suit of Nettles*, then, would seem to bring these associations into focus through Effie, the one goose who especially likes the sideshow. Months earlier she has emerged as a reconciler of opposites, as someone capable of locating a demonic vision in a heavenly and harmonious pattern. Branwell, to use Yeats's terms, is a primary, world-dominated personality who idolizes a creature and composes imagist poems, but Effie, by dying to herself daily, has passed into a life that is beauty. Her poetry is not imagist but visionary and objective; unlike Dorcas, Effie has little of the mirror in her imagination. Finally, the symbol of the Hermaphrodite represents a momentary transcendence of the cyclical, time-dominated order of natural existence described in "September" and, in so doing, reminds the reader that *A Suit of Nettles* moves in two directions, in a pattern of ascent towards intellectual beauty, and round and round in the beautiful, and ugly, world of natural cycles.

The sermon of the drunken preacher is an implicit comment on the whole infernal world described in the country-fair microcosm. It is also a fine piece of prosody, using Anglo-Saxon, four stress accentual meter and both vocalic and consonantal alliteration. The preacher addresses the curious gathering as a leader from the gutter, explaining to them how necessary Judas and all other sinners are to Christ, as Christ himself realized: "Isn't there one, one disciple with the spunk to betray me?" Presumably the text in the background here is St. Paul's "Shall we continue in sin that grace may abound?" (Romans 6:1). Like the child in Reaney's early poem "Antichrist as a Child," Judas is represented as an orphan whose life therefore is marked by violence and self-destruction. As the preacher sees it, the death of Judas on the elder tree closely parallels Christ's on the cross: "His death, his Lord's death held him at Lord's supper." By implication, then, each image of Mome Fair is to help the would-be mental traveler "go through with ghoulish Holy Ghost necessary job" as part of a movement into a redemptive order. The Eclogue comes to a conclusion with the fair gone from sight and attention focused back on the farm in the midst of furious harvest activities, while the wauling of the new baby and the last thunder of the year are heard.

XIII   *The October Eclogue*

After the climactic sights and the crescendo of sound in "September," *A Suit of Nettles* moves quietly towards its conclusion. "December," with its slaughter of the geese, recaptures some of the earlier noise and excitement, but there is nothing equal to the verbal fireworks of the harvest-time passages. Adagio-like, "October," in the form of two lovely lyrics by Branwell and Raymond, is given over to themes favored by Melpomene: disillusionment in love, involving an elegiac identification of the coming of fall and the lover's melancholy; quiet celebration of the savage sweetness of autumnal images, while the "shorter sun sets farther south."

Whatever might have happened through his study of the horse-eating iris to free Branwell, it is immediately evident that his disappointment in love is to be fatal, that life is retreating from him in October as it does from the elm tree leaves. Where Spenser's Cuddie, at this point in the year, has oaten reeds which are rent and worn, Branwell's suit of nettles has turned brown and dry with age. Cuddie claims that it is Colin, not he, who is fit for heavenly poetry, "were he not with loue so ill bedight"; except for Colin's fatal passion he "Would mount as high, and sing as soote as swanne."

Branwell sings sweetly but is still going round in the circles of emotion and passion, not ascending. His lyric suggests the outline of the Orpheus myth, used also in Spenser's "October": "the shepheard, that did fetch his dame / From Plutoes balefull bowre withouten leaue." Branwell tells of his search for a "green woman" in a "green grove" who, like Eurydice, vanished before he could touch her. And now he haunts the place where his vision of loveliness disappeared, making sad lament. One does not have to strain interpretation to see the "Hollow tree" Branwell as a fleeting spirit of nature, holding in harmony, through his music, his natural surroundings, but at the same time threatened by "That which / Trembles heartsmith," by those lovely things in nature, like the leap of a pheasant or of Dorcas, "the gazelle" that cannot be possessed for more than a season.

XIV   *The November Eclogue*

"November" is composed of four thirteen-line stanzas, each one spoken by a different bird. We have seen only one of the birds, Mopsus, before. The topic is the calendar and the question of what point in the changing seasons can accurately be called the year's beginning. "Ookpik," an arctic bird, tells the others that his lord is winter, "The Miller whom none love," who works with the God of Death taking apart men and continents. Frazer's account of the ritual of Adonis includes a description of women lamenting the death of a god of vegetation called Tâ-uz, whose lord ground his bones in a mill (p. 338). The same mythic fancy appears to be working here. Ookpik, though, exults in the way his lord has planned the world in cold arithmetic and grinds everything down to zero. "Starling" hates the cold of winter and believes that the year begins with spring. Once, he tells the others, he inhabited a place of sun (the egg?) and would gladly return there. The "Wildgoose," like the Jews, begins his year in September, the time of his migration southwards. His year contains no winter and has two summers, not four different seasons. The blows of his wings taking him south show him to be a heroic David clearing away the earth's "Goliath snows," in anticipation of the "lord" introduced next by Mopsus.

At this point in the Eclogue we encounter what can only be a major surprise in terms of the book's narrative and characterization. Ookpik's nihilism, Starling's desire to return to the womb, and Wildgoose's heroism in the face of death are followed by a poem in which Mopsus, the philosopher and classicist, emerges as a newly converted believer in Christ and as the one who introduces into the poem the Advent theme. Here too Reaney's sun-myth, repository of a very important complex of images throughout *A Suit of Nettles,* comes to its fulfillment. Mopsus' unnamed lord "is most like a sun for he / Makes his beholders into suns, / Shadowless and timeless." Mopsus, like Effie, now inhabits an order of reality in which shadows and images have been left behind in favor of an objective and eternal truth. The changing seasons, physical struggle, cynicism, and death do not touch the one whose vision is of the lord born a helpless baby on the darkest day of the year but master over all space and time. At this point in *A Suit of Nettles,* with the help of part of the Hercules myth, the theme of mutability is transcended and the possibility of all creation being transformed opens up most completely:

> He crushed the four proud and great directions
> Into the four corners of his small cradle.
> He made it what time of year he pleased, changed
> Snow into grass and gave to all such powers.

The recognition, months before, by Mopsus, of Effie's sibylline character has made it possible for him, if not for Branwell, to pluck a golden bough at her bidding and come out of the world of hellish and purgatorial processes a new creature.

XV *The December Eclogue*

"December" brings the day of Judgment for each goose. The preparation throughout the book has been thorough and the fates of the individual geese are poetically right. Although Branwell and Dorcas, ironically, are chosen by the farm people to keep the race alive, along with Effie, Valancy, and a previously unnamed goose, Old Keziah, George panics and in a neat survival-of-the-physically-fittest kind of move steals the ring which marks Branwell as a survivor. Effie, sacrificial and the exemplar of Christ-like love to the very last, has proven herself the embodiment of efficacious grace in the redemption of Mopsus and now gives her ring to Fanny. Before she and Branwell are swept off into the wild dance of death in which twelve geese a day have dreading hearts severed from dreading minds, they articulate for one last time the two major lines of movement in the whole poem. One involves, as we have seen, symbols of ascent and spiritual progress (ladders and paths), the other symbols of bondage and spiritual defeat (wheels and rings). They are antithetical patterns and the contrast is deliberately left unresolved at the end.

Branwell is perplexed, then fatalistic, when his ring is stolen. Effie, with the best of intentions, again preaches, explaining the crucial point. Her role throughout the poem has prepared for this. She is the main embodiment of ideal pastoral values in the midst of the satire. During her life on the farm she has been a kind of female pastor or shepherdess, caring for the sick and the helpless, giving moral and spiritual instruction, warding off foxes and skunks. Now at the moment of her death she poses the rhetorical question, "Who could be glad to be left alive, who could / Cling to this cramped stupid goosehouse world?" She provides the answer herself, quoting Spenser's Colin (he in turn quotes Chaucer) in the realization that death is not death but an entry into heavenly bliss: "For 'Death's the green pathway' to the fields of Life / 'Die would we daily once it to expert.'"

From Effie's traditional Christian perspective the suit of nettles is the fallen self which must be shed if there is to be salvation. The ring Branwell would cling to is symbolic of life as "a crazed prison of despair." Branwell sees that this ring is identifiable with the merry-go-round and the Ferris wheel, and presumably with all the other manifestations of the cyclical world of nature, but he still wants it. He cannot see a path leading between the head and the body, which prompts Effie's prophecy that his metamorphosis in the next life will be partial; in the language of the Grimms' tale, one arm will always be a goose wing. If Effie is right (the poem, like Duncan judging the bardic contest, never makes an overt decision), Branwell, caught in his own sensual music and like his Brontë prototype, has on the whole failed in his role as mental traveler. The implication, however, is that he will have another opportunity in a subsequent cycle of existence.

A Suit of Nettles is, in its conceptual patterns and major images, and by virtue of the classical English poetic tradition in which it works, a ritualization of the attainment of intellectual or spiritual beauty. It involves a quest whose idealistic values are filtered through ironic and satiric perspectives and also subjected to the criterion of Christian *caritas*. The poem, through its Invocation, announces itself as satire. It is satire, in a very special way, despite the one or two critics who say no. Perhaps the best way of moving towards a definition of the satire is to recognize that *A Suit of Nettles* is a description of two antithetical societies, one composed of crude, unthinking, stock-reflex, sensual creatures, and therefore a fit subject for the satirist's judgment and wrath, the other a civilized community struggling to find itself while it engages in conversations about art, philosophy, and religion, and in making poems.

Branwell, both the tragic hero and a parody of one, is caught between these two worlds. His destruction is delicately balanced emotionally; there is the dignified pathos of Raymond's "This song is like the grapes now / Black in the arbours of fences" and there is the ludicrous figure of melancholy, abused and pushed around by the less sensitively attuned geese. It is one mark of the extraordinary richness and the happy fusion of disparate elements in this poem that Branwell can emerge as both dying god and silly goose.

At the end of *A Suit of Nettles* the fabled world of geese experiencing the culture of the Western world and finally coming to its "Day of wrath and terror" is subsumed into the human world again. The poem ends with a vision of the imagination bursting through the world of nature until, through the agency of divine love, the chaos of water begins to fuse with fire. Then, in Spenserian fashion, the theme of love hovering above both men and geese leads us out into a winter night in the actual historical city of Winnipeg, while the old goose Keziah prepares to lay the eggs from which next year's goslings will come. The process to which the gooseshed belonged has by this time wound part of itself into God, the other part into the cyclical rhythm of history.

XVI "A Message to Winnipeg"

"A Message to Winnipeg" reached its first public through CBC radio in September, 1960, as a program called "Poet and City—Winnipeg," produced by Paul Wright and with musical commentary by John Beckwith. As such, it won an award at the twenty-fifth American Exhibition of Educational Radio and Television with the citation: "A unique wedding of creative talents of the poet and musicians with the intent of a public affairs department. . . . A vivid picturization [sic] of the personality of a city utilizing the qualities peculiar only to radio to stimulate the imagination to the fullest extent."[14] The "Message" has been printed in *Poetry 62*, edited by Eli Mandel and Jean-Guy Pilon, as Reaney's contribution to an anthology of contemporary English and French Canadian poets in whose work Mr. Mandel senses for Canadian society "a gathering of forces for the performance of some unprecedented and enormously significant drama of the mind."[15]

Reaney has also composed two prose sketches about Winnipeg,[16] centering on the idea of a potential Jerusalem at the soul of the historical city. The "Message," in contrast, is primarily a nightmare about a city of destruction, an account of Doomsday coming to the infernal city of the plains. Instead of an imaginative evocation of innocents dancing in the streets, as in the prose sketches, there is squalor, tedium, dehumanization, and pure apocalyptic terror. The "Message" is a technical triumph using ballad patterns, colloquialisms, folk images, commercial slogans, and fractured Métis English, all in the cause of exuberant, devastating satire. Here the sterile land of *A Suit of Nettles* finds its urban counterpart and, although there is little suggested in the way of a green pastoral alternative, one can see the outline of Reaney's characteristic myth. In the handling of time past in the context of time present and time future, there are images of what Winnipeg once was, before the coming of the white man. Even that far back, the landscape was not idyllic, like that of *Twelve Letters* or the idealized parts of *A Suit of*

[114]

Nettles. It was barbaric, a grotesque human form with hair of river grass ten feet tall, a backbone with a crooked silver muddy river, thoughts like ravens in flocks, and legs which were trails. Its blood "was people / Who did what the stars did and the sun."

Since then there have been the French Catholic settlers, who "Had a blood that did what a star did and a Son," and "the Neon People" of the present. It is these last who are the object of wrath, "the human fleas / Of a so-so civilization—half gadget, half flesh," who ritually cut the sacred patterns of commercial produce in factories, while huge Ixion wheels turn, who slaughter children and old ladies with glittering, hard, merciless, and shark-like cars, and who totally ignore the voice of "the poet made up of one thousand rice paper Bible pages." To this poet there comes from the past a kindred voice (another of the "dear bad poets / Who wrote / Early in Canada / And never were of note" mentioned in the *Letters*), that of Pierre Falcon, who in the pre-"Confederation period wrote an anti-"Canadian" ballad:

> Far away and dear, spunky old and early poet
> I wish I could sing the praises of the Neon People
> To You.

Falcon's account of the rout of a troop of English grenadiers is a wild, exuberant fantasy on how the Burnt Wood people whacked and slew and stamped on the lofty invaders.

The poem builds to its message of damnation for Winnipeg; it presents and then rejects an account of life in Winnipeg in terms of the measured, civilized moves of a chess game. No longer is the city what it once seemed, an object of excited curiosity for the poet's questing eye. It is one with the other great cities of the world which gave birth to it. It is a place of Babylonian confusion and spiritual death to which the prophetic messenger, nearly mad with fear, brings a desperate message before he is closed in forever: "Leave this burning city!"

XVII   The Dance of Death at London, Ontario

The Dance of Death at London, Ontario extends Reaney's mental ordering of Canadian locales to another city, the one to which he moved from Winnipeg and in which he has lived since 1960. While a few details of the *Dance* have specifically to do with London, the prosperous "insurance capital" of Ontario, and although all the concrete images are relevant to London, this statement of the poetic macabre could just as well have been made about any place at any time, for the theme is palpably a universal one, the democratic leveling activities of death in any structured society.

The poem opens with an invitation to dance, to the blowing of a trumpet and the beating of a drum. From there it moves through the traffic, buildings, and streets of London, to single out fourteen participants in the dance: the Executive, the Clergyman, the Rich Young Lady, the Woman on the Open Line, the Policeman, the Bride and the Bridegroom, the Grocery Boy, the Scavenger, the Poet and the Painter, and the Doctor. The term "the Clergyman" involves two people, a priest and a minister, who are one in their inane reduction of the great Christian doctrines of faith, hope, and charity to tea-cup chatter. Except for these two, each dancer is treated individually, usually in terms of his or her mental or spiritual state. The image of society which emerges is one of economic injustice, rigid class distinction, luxurious self-indulgence or real poverty, vanished spiritual leadership, and the arts reduced to the level of any other smug middle-class luxury.

Drawings for each section of the poem by Jack Chambers fill in details of the poet's conception and comment wittily on the situation described. In each case the artist has taken a suggestion from the poem and developed it, by having the omnipresent figure of Death undergo a series of changes appropriate to the human individual involved but always remaining indentifiable by his skull face. At one point he is a stiletto-heeled secretary calling the business man to an engagement. At another he wears a shepherd's garb and carries a crook, as he gathers in his sheep behind the backs of the two faithless pastors; they are in full ecclesiastical habit, very Urizenic and decadent, and are served tea by two sheep on hind legs who are adoring society matrons. Still again, Death is a boy on a new suburban sidewalk rolling a hoop (the hoop is Time) with another boy who is waiting for "Cartoon Time" on television. It is one indication of the ironic overtones which encompass the book that the boy who now becomes Death's "newest toy" *is* himself a cartoon figure and in the society in which he lives could never be anything else.

On a slightly more abstract level, each man, woman, and child taken into "this tottery dance" is dead, spiritually and intellectually, before the Angel of Death appears; they too are inhabitants of the sterile land exposed in all Reaney's satires, from the very early time- and death-dominated lyrics to his major poems like *A Suit of Nettles*.

The structure of ironic myth and satire is a parody of romance, the application of romantic verbal structures to more realistic contents. It is not difficult to see how the relatively inexperienced twenty-year-old Red Heart poet, attracted to themes of love blotted out by nihilistic ones of death and destruction had already, by 1947-49, hit upon the basic myth which was to inform his mature satires fifteen or twenty years later. In the interval there has been an extraordinary growth in prosodic skill and in intellectual consciousness but the weeds, rats, autumn leaves, and bats are still working as the sinister background for the baby at the gates of life.

Something new has been added, however, since the days of *The Red Heart*. The baby who emerges at the end of *The Dance of Death* tells Death that it will dance, but not in dread, for it knows of a "Holy One" who someday will shut up Death's book. It is this part of the story that concerns Reaney in his pastoral comedies, dealt with in Chapter Three of this book. Reaney tells us on the back cover of *The Dance of Death* that the idea for it came from an old German *totentanz* book, *The Dance of Death at Basle,* and also from seeing some burdocks in an old graveyard at the edge of the city. These were the immediate causes, perhaps. The myth was working much earlier, taking various shapes, but also waiting for this most skeletal one.

CHAPTER 3

The Earth in the Arms of the Sun

REANEY'S interest in drama reaches back to his childhood experiences in school plays and to attendance at a performance of the Dramatic Society at the Stratford Normal School where his mother took her teacher training. His own dramatic creations, however *avant garde* they are in some ways, maintain an unbroken and very valuable imaginative connection with small-town and school theater. Early in his career, the suitability of much of his poetry for oral presentaion was recognized; the "Great Lakes Suite" from *The Red Heart* was adapted for CBC radio with a musical setting by John Beckwith. In January, 1958, towards the conclusion of his doctoral studies in English at the University of Toronto, Reaney brought a kind of dramatic and satiric sense out of the experience of reading the vast list of selections formerly provided by the Department of English for the General Examinations. This took the form of a play with the cliché title *From "Beowulf" to Virginia Woolf*. It was staged by the Graduate English Club for an audience of about one hundred university people and was very much a literary man's spoof for a group of initiates also caught up in the same graduate school mysteries.

In the same year, a reading on the radio of two of the eclogues from *A Suit of Nettles* induced Pamela Terry, who was to be the director of his two first public productions, to comment on "the extremely workable *aural* readability" of the two eclogues and to urge him to write for the theater.[1] As it turned out, Reaney was already at work on a play called *The Rules of Joy* which later, after much rewriting and shortening, became the comedy *The Sun and the Moon*. Even before this, as early as 1953, the libretto for the opera *Night-blooming Cereus* had begun to take shape, although it was not ready for performance until March, 1959, on "CBC Wednesday Night."

From these early beginnings Reaney has considerably expanded his experience as a dramatist and is now widely recognized as the writer to whom many are looking as one of the brightest hopes in the dark annals of Canadian playwriting. To date his reputation as dramatist has been formed mainly on the basis of *The Killdeer,* a comedy written in 1959 and given four productions since: by the University Alumnae Dramatic Club, Toronto, in 1960; by the CBC, for their prestigious "Festival" television series in 1961; by the BBC for their "Third Programme"; by the Glasgow Citizen's Theatre in Scotland, as part of the Commonwealth Arts Festival, in 1965. As well as having had these various productions, *The Killdeer* is one of the only four Reaney dramas published to date; the other three are *The Sun and the Moon, One-man Masque,* and *Night-blooming Cereus. The Sun and the Moon* so far has had only an amateur production by the Campus Players at London, Ontario, in the summer of 1965. *One-man Masque* has been performed twice by the author, in Hart House Theatre, Toronto, in 1960, and later in the Unitarian Church in Hamilton, Ontario; it was also played by Jeremy Wilkin on CBC-TV's "Q for Quest" in 1961. *Night-blooming Cereus* has reached a wide Canadian audience, through two radio performances on "CBC Wednesday Night," in 1959 and 1960, and as a stage production, part of a double-bill along with the *Masque,* in Hart House in the spring of 1960. These four compositions merit close study by anyone wishing to understand Reaney's writings but they are now only part of the story of his work for the theater.

In this chapter and the following one, individual plays are located in the wider context of dramatic activity provided by Reaney's unpublished and, in some cases, unproduced works for the theater. Equally important, the plays are set in the total context of Reaney's writings to date. The recent play *Listen to the Wind,* with its poetic riches and its extraordinary theatrical effectiveness, and in spite of what some feel to be too long a playing time, rivals *The Killdeer* for first place among the plays to date. It is the first of the full-length plays directed by Reaney himself. In addition there are a comedy *(The Easter Egg),* the libretto for another opera *(The Shivaree),* a children's play *(Names and Nicknames),* a play for children with music by Alfred Kunz *(Let's Make a Carol),* two marionette plays *(Little*

Red Riding Hood, Apple Butter), and two parts of a three-part verse and music collage done in collaboration with John Beckwith for the CBC as part of the Canadian Centennial Celebrations. (Another play for adults, *The Three Desks*, has been completed, but is so far unread by me.)

Before plunging into interpretation and correlation of Reaney's dramatic writings, it seems desirable to take stock of the kind of poet it is who in recent years has increasingly made writing for the theater his main task. It is clear that the delightfully casual quality of much of the literature in the Reaney corpus covers a consciously used and highly unified structure of symbols as well as thoroughly learned skills in prosody. We have looked at various aspects of the latter (someone might well do a much more detailed study of the metrics of Reaney's art) and we have seen his symbolic structure taking shape from the time of the earliest works. With the publication, in 1958, of *A Suit of Nettles*, after seven years of university teaching and further studies in classical English and American literature, it was clear that in several senses Reaney had come of age. *A Suit of Nettles* could not have been written without these intervening literary experiences. It is evident, however, that the poetic sensibility and freshness and the highly individual vision of *The Red Heart* were still very much there. The study of Chaucer, Spenser, Blake, the Brontës, and Yeats—and a host of other writers less influential on him—had in no sense demolished or overwhelmed him. It seems rather to have provided a heightened awareness of what he himself had been doing earlier and a growth in knowledge of all the many things he might now do in the particular Canadian environment which still intensely held his interest.

Reaney, like many other Canadians, at one time considered becoming an expatriate artist, but it seems never to have been a significant temptation. Other than a short stay in England and a brief visit to Scotland for the production of *The Killdeer*, he has stayed away from Europe. Similarly, he has never felt himself drawn to the U. S. A. as a possible place to live. It might be thought by those who scorn love of country in favor of jet set internationalism that this would simply lead to provincialism and irrelevance for the world at large in what he writes. Certainly Reaney himself, from childhood on, has been aware of the possible constricting influences of small-town and country life, as the short stories and poems like "The Upper Canadian" show. His way of handling the problem, however, was not to export himself elsewhere but rather to learn an order of words or literary language comprehensive enough to swallow up the place and society which had brought him into being, and in the process to make himself capable of writing satire, romance, and comedy of a kind not written before in the Canadian environment. The exuberant farce about small-town gossip in the early scenes of *The Killdeer* and the fulfillment of romantic longings of people in Shakespeare, Ontario, described in *Night-blooming Cereus,* have permanently set free certain parts of Canadian existence and given them a reality which they could never have had outside of art. At the same time these are works which have what is usually called "universal" appeal.

The two other major influences working on Reaney during the 'fifties and 'sixties have been the literary criticism of Northrop Frye and the practical demands of writing for musical settings and stage productions. We shall return to the second of these a little later. Frye's now enormous influence in the literary culture of North America and beyond had its beginning, as most Canadian academics know, with the publication of *Fearful Symmetry: A Study of William Blake,* and has continued to grow, through his teaching of undergraduates and graduates at Victoria College in the University of Toronto, by means of visiting lectureships at dozens of universities in North America and in Britain, through a host of critical articles on a very wide range of literary and cultural topics, in convocation addresses, and through the publication of books on Milton, T. S. Eliot, Shakespeare, and others. Paramount among his writings is the amazing intellectual *tour-de-force, Anatomy of Criticism: Four Essays* (1957), a work of theoretical literary criticism which in recent years appears to have provided more working hypotheses for students of literature than any other critical work of our time.

Except in conversations with friends from Victoria College, Reaney, who was at University College, did not come under the influence of Frye as an undergraduate in the 'forties. He had gone into English Language and Literature, as he tells it, to study *Wuthering Heights*. Not surprisingly, then, his immersion in the context of the sound traditional and historical scholarship of University College's Department of English was a kind of disciplining experience to which he reacted fairly violently, even to the point of transferring to Classics at Trinity College for a two-week period, at the end of which he went back to English. Although he now expresses admiration for much that was taught him at University College, he has no doubt that his intellectual awakening came when, during his early years of teaching at the University of Manitoba, he read and began to live with *Fearful Symmetry* and the poetry of Blake. Predictably, then, it was the presence of Frye in Toronto which brought him there for doctoral study in 1956.

Although there are still many readers of poetry who firmly believe that the influence of literary criticism, theoretical or practical, can only be inimical to a poet's development, such does not appear to have been the case with Reaney's learning from Frye. Those acquainted with Frye's writings will recognize that his is the kind of criticism which can in a profound way be a shaping and liberating experience for artists as well as for others. At the same time, what a poet like Reaney comes up against in reading *Fearful Symmetry* or *Anatomy of Criticism* is fundamentally an invitation to immerse himself in the classics of literature in the English language. All the exciting speculative and more hypothetical parts of Frye's criticism are secondary to this in importance. And this, it seems clear, is the way in which Reaney reacted. I believe that he is one of the few Toronto Ph.D.'s in English who claim at some time in their lives to have read pretty well everything stipulated on the old (it is now considerably revised) General Examinations Reading List. The directing of Reaney into intensive English studies might have taken place even without Frye's influence but it is clear to one who knows the work of the two of them that the quality and direction of Reaney's reading experience would have been vastly different without it, which brings us to the second major Reaney debt to Frye.

In 1949, the year of the publication of *The Red Heart* and still before *Fearful Symmetry* had begun to work on him, Reaney wrote a master's thesis on the novels of Ivy Compton-Burnett which he now dismisses contemptuously as mainly plot-summary, because he feels he did not at that time know anything about literary structure. It is this knowledge which he claims to have gained from Frye. But this is an over-simplification, if my reading of the early pieces is not completely wrong-headed. It is true that in his apprentice years he worried about the problem of structure a good deal; having written a novel each summer of his undergraduate period, he then abandoned the manuscripts because he felt them to be structurally weak. This suggests that it was structure in the sense of a large design which was the problem. When he encountered Frye's principles of archetypal symbolism and typology, he felt himself free to attempt the sustained patterning evident in the complex *A Suit of Nettles.*

But one can see another kind of critical principle working in the early lyrics and short stories, a principle which Frye himself also articulates, although Reaney appears to have had no conscious knowledge of it that early. This is the principle of the discontinuous poem,[2] which, in Frye's view, underlies the work of the *symboliste* poets in France as well as those writing in English who were influenced by them, like the early Yeats. According to this principle, "poetic images do not state or point to anything, but, by pointing to each other, they suggest or evoke the mood which informs the poem." This is not to suggest a classifying, in any narrow sense, of the early Reaney pieces as *symbolistes.* They are, as we have seen, imagistic, given over to the creation of a world of fantasy, of wallpaper and marionettes, of nightmares and romantic longings. One can observe developing in them an overall antithesis between the nightmare world and that of pluperfect things which has remained to this day and is centrally important in the plays.

Still, the early writings are, in the main, discontinuous, separate lyrics or short stories concerned with the creation of a self-sustained mood. It is not without significance that the ordering of the forty-two poems in *The Red Heart* volume was not done by Reaney himself, but was the work of Colleen Thibaudeau (later his wife) and Sybil Hutchinson (his literary agent since 1949). The larger construct is there, nevertheless, and the world of the Red Heart is palpable and realized. Despite the early

[123]

incapacity for sustained narrative or architectonic design, one can see a potential for the handling of large symbols not tied to the individual, subjective moods of the artist. If Reaney learned from Frye and from poets of the large design, it is because he was already aware of a problem and was trying to solve it. At one point in his doctoral dissertation[3] he makes this comment on a passage from Yeats's *The Wanderings of Oisin:* ". . . we feel the archetype being smothered in a quickstand of prettiness and private imagery." This seems to be the way his own search, in the 'fifties and 'sixties, for what he calls "a possible grammar of symbols" has led him to think of his own earlier work. It does not mean, of course, that the reader or critic has to follow the poet in reacting against the early pieces. It does not mean even that Reaney himself has disowned them (he would like to see a new edition of them). It is simply a matter of his growth as a writer. It is undoubtedly true, moreover, that the meanings of the juvenilia have accumulated with each successive later composition, but still they do exist in their own right and have their own vitality.

A careful study of *A Suit of Nettles* brings the realization that relatively few symbols organize everything else in a Reaney composition. In this long poem we have the creation of an imaginative landscape, which turns out to be a mental one, in which patterns of ascent (spirals and ladders) and patterns of recurrence (wheels and rings) predominate. This landscape can justly be called "Reaneyland," in that it is not any actual place or places but draws on several. It is a thoroughly realized imaginative construct within which the central figure is the youthful poet or artist, flanked by two other kinds of figures, the brutal or indifferent adult and the Christlike counselor. This last figure may, as in the case of Effie, be female. Other figures tend to divide into two groups, those impeding the poet's growth and those assisting it. If he is to proceed to a higher level of being, to an integration of heart and mind, the influence of the wise counselors must prevail. Since *A Suit of Nettles* is written mainly in a minor key, Branwell (like his Brontë forebear) remains caught in his infernal world and goes down to destruction in a communal *danse macabre*. He is also like the youthful Yeats, needing the help of Lady Gregory to build the ladder leading up

[124]

to the mind from the "foul rag-and-bone shop of the heart." He is the Red Heart, making poems from a small and personal world but finally frustrated in all his desires because he as yet has no way of entry into what Reaney, in his essay on Isabella Valancy Crawford, calls "the world of great poetry formed by the impersonal literary imagination itself" (p. 268).

Nonetheless, *A Suit of Nettles* marks a major advance from the early poems and short stories, through its careful description of the means of spiritual and mental progress. In so doing it is a fable about unrealized possibilities. Reaney has given to Branwell only as much of his total imagination as will fit into the miniature form of the pastoral eclogue. The boy-poet in *Twelve Letters*, since he appears in a landscape far less filled with potential menace, is moving towards maturity, while the Old Man and the Old Woman look down, guarding his world with their ancestral wisdom. Reaney's central myth concerns the quest for one's true parents or the rebirth of the soul; this involves recognition of all the possible obstacles, both within and without the poet-protagonist's self, which may impede that quest. The dramas, since most of them are pastoral comedies, show the goal as achieved or as about to be, thus completing the process begun in the Red Heart's wanderings and brought to the verge of completion in Branwell's.

I   The Killdeer

Anyone present at the opening of Reaney's first fully produced comedy, *The Killdeer*, will not easily forget the excitement it engendered in the Coach House Theatre. Through a dazzling array of poetic language, excellent acting parts, and bizarre psychological unravellings one soon realized that *The Red Heart*, that intensely private book of problems stated but not resolved, had come to the stage. The destructive Sundogs, with their laying waste of nature, had combined with the English orphan—and also with Jezebel, the Whore of Babylon, and Malory's Morgan la Fay—to create Madam Fay, a cosmetic saleswoman making her lurid passage through a rural Ontario cultural backwater. There was also the emerging boy-poet, afraid to leave behind his toys and childhood games because of the horror of the adult world, and wishing, "If only we could choose our fathers and mothers." There were enough dominating parental figures to keep small boys running down leafless lanes of fear forever. But several of the redemptive elements brought together in *A Suit of Nettles* had combined with *The Red Heart* and resolutions had been worked out.

The first act of *The Killdeer* sets the theme, the necessity of the young freeing themselves from slavery to their parents, if they are to mature, and the extreme reluctance of the parents to let this happen. The protagonist is Harry Gardner, an acne'd unprepossessing young man dominated by his fussy, pious, bossy mother. Her refrain is "I feel I don't know my boy's heart any longer" or, when addressing Harry himself, "I wish you'd open your heart to me," to which he replies, "When I'm asleep / Why don't you take off the top of my head / And put your hand in? What could I show you / Mother, except yourself?" He believes that if he could only get married, he'd be all right, and the girl who is obviously the one for him, the egg-girl Rebecca from near the Huckleberry Marsh, is already known to him. But certain complex matters make this union unlikely, at least for the present, and Act I ends with both Harry and Rebecca going to marry someone else. Act II shows the disastrous consequences, and Act III restores sanity to what has by then been revealed as a very sick world.

Harry's situation is bad, but it is ideal compared with Rebecca's. It is Madam Fay who briefs Mrs. Gardner and the audience on Rebecca's background and on her own, in a thoroughly arresting expository scene. This background is so rich in grotesque detail that Mrs. Gardner, who has never used cosmetics in her life, buys several, just to keep the painted lady in the cottage to feed her hunger for salaciousness. We learn that Madam Fay, "vital, pagan, and dressed in an elegant blouse with a dark skirt stylishly gored in front," has a son Eli who is nineteen and hates her; she has left his upbringing to the hired man Clifford who, we learn later, has exercised a sinister hold over the boy ever since his childhood. Years ago Madam Fay, married to Eli's father and having tried "to virgin up a bit before her marriage," ran away to Buffalo for a weekend with her sister's husband Lorimer. As a result her husband shot Lorimer's family, all except a girl (we learn later that this is Rebecca) who since then has run the farm alone. The murderer of Rebecca's family is in the mental hospital at London, taking his bed apart and putting it together again, a suitable enough fate for the man who unwittingly married the Whore of Babylon. Madam Fay now travels the country roads in a pink Baby Austin with silver curlicues and purple plush inside, selling "beauty," with the story of her past for bait when sales are poor. Sizing up Mrs. Gardner as a church-going biddy, she tells her,

> You'd buy
> The rouge pot Jezebel used the day she was tossed
> Off her balcony to the dogs just to see
> The woman that caused four deaths and one
> Of the splatteriest nervous breakdowns I ever saw
> And one blighted boy—my son—and one blighted girl—
> My sister's daughter.

When Rebecca arrives later in Act I to deliver Mrs. Gardner's eggs, she announces that she is to be married the next day to Eli Fay, this having been arranged by Clifford. By now Harry, who is a clerk in the local branch of the Royal Bank of Canada, has been needed to fill an empty chair at the banker's dinner party. While there he has got rather drunk, never before having been "tempted by alcohol," as his mother puts it, and in the rather confused events which follow has been proposed to by the banker's daughter Vernelle. On returning home he hears of Rebecca's plans and realizes that he has lost her, still having learned about her only that her favorite bird is the killdeer. Under his mother's prodding, and although he'd "like to be a tramp / Or work on a farm or maybe both and read / Difficult books on easy haystacks," he returns to tell Vernelle he will marry her.

Now all this sounds as if Reaney had collected the skeletons of an entire rural community's memory over a period of twenty years and brought them together in one tale. Certainly the play is in several essentials unabashedly melodramatic. It would be naive theater fare after the first few minutes if it were not set forth in some of the most exuberant, image-filled language an audience could ask for, a language which permits a probing into human beings which is anything but naive. Mr. Mavor Moore, reviewing the first production for the Toronto *Telegram*, had this verdict:

> For when the history of the Canadian theatre comes to be written, I should not be at all surprised to find *The Killdeer* listed as the first Canadian play of real consequence, and the first demonstration of genius among us. . . . The great thing is that the words Mr. Reaney has written for Miss Terry and her actors soar, spin, whirl and flash like nothing ever heard on our stage before. And he rips us open as people with a sort of jolly whimsy which may forever mark the end of the myth of the stolid, sober, inarticulate Canadian.

The characters, stereotyped in abstract, have all the life that vital use of words can give them. To a high degree they are metaphorically conceived. As Harry, for example, changes and develops, there are several "I am you" equations: first he *is* his mother, then Vernelle, and finally Rebecca. Similarly, Eli moves from Clifford to Harry, and eventually starts to break free of both.

In *A Suit of Nettles* the characters in Reaneyland are birds with human natures, as in the traditional bestiary or beast fable. In *The Killdeer* the characters are human with bird or beast characteristics. Clifford, an orphan like Madam Fay, is described as the cowbird which lays its egg in another's nest and tries to push out the true child. In Ryder Haggard's *Dawn*, a favorite novel for Reaney from the age of eight and the source of much of the plot for the inner play of *Listen to the Wind*, there is a cowbird-orphan character, Douglas, whose lust for the possession of property and the souls of the innocent closely parallels Clifford's. Clifford's victim is Eli, described as a bunny or lamb.

The play has many such images. Mrs. Gardner and her friend Mrs. Budge, both rich comic creations who take on a peculiar pathos as the play develops, are on one level "Two old crows / Gliding over the spring fields trying to pry out / Where that delicious decaying smell is from" or "a pair of old hens in the barnyard / Chasing a bit of thrown-away dirty meat. . . ." Before Rebecca's arrival they try, with the help of elderblossom wine, to piece together the whole macabre tale read years ago in the newspaper. They dart about the stage—shrieking, cawing vultures circling over bits of carrion.

[128]

When Rebecca goes away, she leaves behind her two brown paper silhouettes of Eli and Clifford, the groom-to-be and the best man; she has taken these to town as measurements for the wedding suits. Almost struck dumb by Rebecca's disclosure that she is marrying the son of the man who killed her mother and two brothers, the son of the woman who comitted adultery with her father, Mrs. Gardner and Mrs. Budge drain their glasses of wine, seize the papermen, cry out that their partners are stark naked, and, in one of the play's most theatrically effective scenes, dance.

With Act II the tone of *The Killdeer* changes abruptly. As the curtain rises, to the sound of a killdeer cry, Rebecca has been sentenced to hang for the murder and mutilation of Clifford. Several years have passed and a great deal has changed in "the river of time" sung about by Mrs. Budge. The exuberant farce of Act I is far in the distance, as the play moves into something close to dark conceit or allegory. Rebecca emerges as a sacrificial victim (Madam Fay calls her "a female Jesus"), having confessed to a crime she thought was Eli's. Harry, now a graduate of Osgoode Hall Law School and married to Vernelle, has returned to his home village to practice law. He is soon involved in an attempt to rescue Rebecca from the consequences of her actions. To do so he manages to persuade the Jailer's wife, a Mrs. Soper, who hates being wife to a bunch of keys and longs to help the innocent prisoner, to let him into Rebecca's cell. There, in the erotic climax of the comedy, a child is conceived so that, as Harry has planned, a stay of execution is granted until after the birth of the baby, by which time a new trial has been arranged.

Act III is given over mainly to this second trial, at which a sudden revelation of facts hitherto unknown by almost everyone exonerates Rebecca. The play ends with Eli making the first steps towards adulthood after many years of infantile regression. The two necessary divorces will be arranged, so that Rebecca and Harry can be married, and since it is they who have enabled Eli reluctantly to give up his toys, they are to be his foster parents.

The Killdeer, despite widespread plaudits, has been criticized on several counts, as not presenting a unified action, as containing unstageworthy dialogue, as resorting to techniques of exposition inadequately mastered, and, above all, as proceeding on several levels—naturalistic, fantastic, and symbolic—which fail to coincide, with the result that the horrific acts round which the play evolves cannot be taken seriously by the audience. These, clearly, are strong charges and need examination.

First, let it be said that I too (on the first night and for a time afterwards), despite a strong conviction that *The Killdeer* really was something rare and theatrically rich, was bothered by the way in which an ostensible naturalism seemed to wrestle uneasily with symbolic meanings and with the over-simplifications of character and event expected in melodrama. This tendency became really serious, it seemed, in Act III. I have later concluded, for reasons I shall come to, that my reaction was at least partially wrong. Part of the trouble was, more than likely, simply a matter of audience unreadiness for an arresting new voice in the theater. Be that as it may, Reaney has done a good deal of rewriting, at various stages, of the troublesome third act of *The Killdeer*, since he in all humility does take seriously the necessity for recognizing the practical demands of live theater and is not, as two early critics claimed, an accomplished lyric poet trying to exploit a medium which he is unwilling to come to grips with. The result of the rewriting, however, has been a justified return to the early version; this is the one published in 1962.

The question of whether the dialogue and exposition in *The Killdeer* (or in other Reaney dramas) are stageworthy or not can be determined finally, one supposes, only in terms of audience response. This has always been mixed in the extreme, ranging from genuine, unforced delight at the verbal wit, the inventiveness, and the poetic resonances to embarassment and disgust with the way a Reaney play ingenuously asks you to surrender to its apparently wayward fancies and arbitrariness. One gathers, moreover, from the generally enthusiastic reviews of *The Killdeer* when it played in Britain, and even though a few of them show the old uneasiness with the melodramatic elements, that the much-discussed Canadian self-hatred in matters of the native theater has worked strongly against *The Killdeer*. Perhaps also there is the question of a British audience's greater capacity for responding in the theater to verbal iconography. In any case it is clear that several of the British reviewers understood far more of what *The Killdeer* is than did most of their Canadian counterparts. (The annotated Bibliography at the end of this book contains the substance of these reviews.)

The key to what went wrong with the play in Canada can be found in Reaney's "August Eclogue," in the critical attitude burlesqued there as one so intent on deciding whether a new piece of literary art is good or bad and whether or not it uses "real language of the people" that no time is taken to ask the primary question, "What kind of work is it?" *The Killdeer* is a comedy. Its plot structure in its essentials could not be more conventional, in the ways described by Northrop Frye in his now widely known account of how comedies are put together. Since Reaney in this play and in some of the others is clearly influenced by Frye's theory, as well as by his own knowledge of actual comedies, I give the basic part of it here:

> What normally happens is that a young man wants a young woman, that his desire is resisted by some opposition, usually paternal, and that near the end of the play some twist in the plot enables the hero to have his will. In this simple pattern there are several complex elements. In the first place, the movement of comedy is usually a movement from one kind of society to another. At the beginning of the play the obstructing characters are in charge of the play's society, and the audience recognizes that they are usurpers. At the end of the play the device in the plot that brings hero and heroine together causes a new society to crystallize around the hero, and the moment when this crystallization occurs is the point of resolution in the action, the comic discovery, *anagnorisis* or *cognitio*.[4]

The final society reached by the comedy is the one recognized throughout by the audience as the desirable one, the one towards which the audience looks and even, in terms of the theatrical illusion, helps to bring about. The obstacles to the hero's desire form the action of the comedy and are usually parental, as in *The Killdeer*. As these are removed, one by one, the play achieves its resolution. Since, moreover, the tendency of comedy is to include as many as possible of its characters in the new society at the end, there normally are several unlikely conversions whereby those blocking characters who have made the dramatic action possible through the conflict they engender are brought into harmony with those they earlier have opposed. All this fits the plot structure of *The Killdeer* like a glove.

It is a little further on in the description that we come to an idea which helps to explain the troubles to date with *The Killdeer*. Frye says,

> There are two ways of developing the form of comedy: one is to throw the main emphasis on the blocking characters; the other is to throw it forward on the scenes of discovery and reconciliation. One is the general tendency of comic irony, satire, realism, and studies of manners; the other is the tendency of Shakespearean and other types of romantic comedy.[5]

Both Canadian productions of *The Killdeer* to date have fallen into the trap of playing it as if it were, in the main, the former kind of play, when in fact it is the latter and was, I think, consciously written as such. Although I did not see the Glasgow production, it appears from descriptions of it that Mr. David William was not tricked by the play into treating it as a comedy of rural Ontario manners. This left him free to look at the work as an imaginative construct in its own right and as having, finally, little more to do with actual Stratford, Ontario, environs than Shakespeare's *As You Like It* has to do with an identifiable late sixteenth-century England.

In fairness to those who have found the Canadian moral of the play irresistible, it needs to be admitted that there is a good deal in *The Killdeer* which can be read this way. When the blocking characters have the exuberant vitality of a Madam Fay or the sinister menace of a Clifford, it is not easy, one imagines, for a director and actors to keep an audience's attention focused towards a comic ending which must include the routing of these characters. There is almost nothing, moreover, in Canadian theater which even approaches Reaney's plays in their capacity to swallow the raw materials of existence in this country and transform them into that something quite different which I call Reaneyland. Perhaps this is one thing which distinguishes a major writer from a lesser one, the capacity to let his vision of an imaginative reality take shape and assert itself in a variety of works, regardless of the trammels of environment which would, if permitted, pull it down again.

Reaney's activities here are the precise opposite of what used to be called "the maple leaf school" of Canadian literature. For all his interest in things Canadian, it is clear that the major impetus is the desire to induce others to escape the dreary actuality of the environment. There are many lines with which to illustrate this, but perhaps Madam Fay, a very authentic denizen of Reaneyland, in her attempt to sell her "Jezebel" lipstick to the reluctant and inhibited Minnie Gardner, puts it best: "Doesn't the maple leaf / Turn red in the fall?" Doesn't a sufficient measure of outrageous artistic recreation make even the dull Canadian facts glow with excitement?

It is poetic power above all else which makes significant *The Killdeer's* reworking of the structure of archetypal comedy. The play, if interpreted to any large extent as naturalism, is made to fight with its own poetic genius and, in the process, to appear disunited. In fact its action proceeds almost entirely on another level, that of myth and symbol; we are not meant to take seriously the horrific acts, except as they are vested with meaning on this other level.

The play is held together by a carefully worked out pattern of interlocking images. As with most Reaney compositions, the central unifying symbol is in the title. Rebecca is the killdeer, the bird which cries out over towns just before a storm and which will also attract an enemy to itself to lead it away from the young ones in the nest. Eli is several times described as a bird who has not yet learned to fly. Through Harry's years of marriage to the vulture Vernelle, among the vultures of Osgoode Hall Law School, he carries in his wallet a killdeer feather. As a child, Madam Fay once killed the killdeer of her foster sister, Rebecca's mother, in an attempt at least to evoke hatred for herself, since she felt unloved; hence the attempt at revenge, by stealing her sister's husband. Eli too, as a boy, once found a dead killdeer in the pasture and was knocked down, kicked, and cursed by his mother when he showed it to her. As Harry slowly pieces together all this information, in the manner of a detective story, he is led to conclude that a dead killdeer showed suddenly to Madam Fay in court may break her, to the point of telling what she knows of Clifford's death. And this is how it turns out, although what Harry and the court learn is not what they expect.

The killdeer has its symbolic opposite. In a semi-allegorical scene in Act II Harry fights for the life of the woman "sentenced on a Friday, to be hanged in September." Rebecca has seen her marriage to Eli as potentially "love's solution to the puzzle of hatred," an Effie-like notion, but like Branwell, Harry is convinced only slowly that hate does not win. To get to Rebecca, who will teach him this truth, he must defeat a Mr. Manatee, a hangman descendant of all the sterile destroying figures in Reaney's earlier works. Mr. Manatee craves the luxury of annihilating life and performing abortions on the soul. His name *manatee* denotes a marine animal, indicating, it would seem, that this is another variant in Reaney's use of the traditional destroying sea-monster from bestiary tradition. Mr. Manatee is the brother of Death and has a farm in a land of darkness

> My farm was in the County of Night and grew nothing
> But fields of nightshade and bladder campion,
> Gardens of burdocks. Mandrakes in the haymows.
> I fed my cattle on such fare as made their udders
> Run black blood and their wombs bear freemartens.
> I raised weasels in my henhouses and I
> Set traps for barley but bred rats who
> Ate the little pigs as they lay sucking the sow.

The hangman rejoices that the little bird Rebecca will swing into his noose without effort, "Like the pet bird with a broken wing that knows / You're going to help it."

Here the theme of sterility, part of the larger theme of growth and maturity, emerges most strongly. Against Mr. Manatee, Harry resolves to pit his phallic powers, believing that only a new life can serve as an adequate human weapon against the death principle. This is the core of meaning in *The Killdeer*. The tangle of perverted sexual and familial patterns— oedipal attachments, adultery, murder, homosexuality, mutilation, and others—all come together in the figure of Mr. Manatee. In the context of the fertility theme all these perversions *are*

[134]

death, annihilation, the refusal to do battle against the evil which haunts the world like a destroying monster.

Against Mr. Manatee and what he represents, Harry and Rebecca, working together, have a limited success. The real resolution, which permits the emergence of a new order, comes through the advent into the play in the last act of the mysterious Dr. Ballad. Having been the village doctor for years, he is now a hermit in a little hut in the center of the swamp near the Fay and Lorimer farms. No communication with the outside world is the rule of his house, and he enters the courtroom symbolically carrying a bouquet of wild-grass leaves.

Dr. Ballad is a man for all seasons; having already lived a useful social existence, he now spends his years watching tracks in the snow, sedges, grasses and flowers, or clouds and butterflies. He records all in his journal. Now, in his brief re-entry into society as the play's exemplar of mature love and wisdom, he is pitted against the order of legalism represented by the Judge, who also keeps a journal, but one filled with "all the crimes committed in this country, / All the robberies, incests, rapes, murders." The prosaic, legalistic mind of the Judge does not understand Dr. Ballad's oblique explanation of the rotting horse image, which has appeared intermittently throughout the play. This is an important speech, concerned with reconciliation of the violent clashing of opposites which have made the play's action; Dr. Ballad feels that it would be most interesting if the leaves in both their diaries were interwoven: "flowers and butterflies, grass / Growing from the dead horse's body in the ditch."

Dr. Ballad is an emancipated spirit who now briefly has to be caught in the swamp of human misery if redemption is to be possible. Having told Eli that he must abandon childhood toys, he heralds the coming of a new reality: "The heron / Flies slowly over the marsh from the farm of / Darkness to the farm of light." In some mysterious way he both knows and can liberate each of Eli, Rebecca, and Harry at the play's end:

> I know all your stories and see the order of their tanglings.
> Like a butterfly in the glitter haze of the marsh
> The entanglement weighs me down—but I cross,
> I fly on, I disentangle, I release you all.

The quest for true parents has led round and round in the circles of neurosis and corrupt nature until gradually images of aspiration—killdeers, moths, butterflies, hawks, a stair of darkness on the way to light, a tower of air—have come to dominate the play. The ideal world towards which *The Killdeer* moves earlier has existed only in the mind of Rebecca and, to some extent, in that of Mrs. Soper. Now, as the Judge leaves the court and Dr. Ballad wanders into the Judge's desk, the rule of charity succeeds that of law and the allegory of the play is quietly and unobtrusively complete.

II   The Sun and the Moon

The Sun and the Moon, written before *The Killdeer* but not produced until 1965, and *The Easter Egg,* written last of the three, contain several by now familiar characters. The Effie-Rebecca figure returns, with her vision of a better world, and is especially important in redeeming the youthful male protagonist in *The Easter Egg.* There is a sensitive, esthetic youth in each play, reluctant or unable until the end to give up his childish fantasies and embrace the ambiguities and difficulties of the adult world. And Madam Fay is back, changed but recognizable, as the woman deprived in her childhood of the necessary love to grow up, and turned, therefore, into a sadist preying on the weak.

The Sun and the Moon has not the same degree of metaphorical extravagance and poetic richness that *The Killdeer* has. Although far from simple, the story line is not as complex as that of *The Killdeer* and the action is more obviously unified. Again, the manners and morals of a rural Ontario community provide a point of departure for the satire and farce necessary to shake up the conventional processes of those both off- and on-stage. After this loosening-up process, romantic comedy, using symbolic means to achieve its end, takes over.

The play, on its most literal level, is set at Millbank, Ontario, in the year 1935. With great gusto and a keen sense of the absurd, it tears apart the pieties and pretensions of the local United Church congregation, it plays havoc with the sexual habits of the natives, and it brings the formerly quiet little town into a state of awareness that it won't forget in many a year.

Reaney's most useful agent in all this is the exuberant, mischief-making Mrs. Charlotte Shade, who arrives in town to set the action going. Her connotations are many. She claims to be, but isn't, the former teen-age mistress of the Reverend Francis Kingbird of the United Church. She is a high-class abortionist and charlatan from Toronto, on the run from those who would bring her to justice. She passes herself off as an evangelist devoted especially to the help and salvation of young girls in trouble and, like Chaucer's demagogic Pardoner, makes ample use of lurid confessional rhetoric in the hoodwinking of her ignorant and gullible listeners in the Millbank Women's Institute. On the level of allegory indicated in her name she is linked with Beelzebub, Antichrist, and the archetypal fire-dragon. Antithetically, Kingbird is the repository of all that, in this play, is good and Christlike. He is a kind, loving parent, he is intellectually enlightened, and he is unmoved when the whirlwind hits him. His kingdom is as far, spiritually, from that of Mrs. Shade as is the sun from the moon. Unlike his *Killdeer* counterpart, Dr. Ballad, Kingbird plays a major role throughout the play, with the result that the forces of destruction and darkness never have as much control as they do throughout most of *The Killdeer*.

With an almost hagiographic abstraction the allegory of the two kingdoms works itself out, through sets of interlocking images to do with the summer solstice, death and resurrection, and souls fought for and won or lost. Around Kingbird and Mrs. Shade a group of young men and women grope towards love and happiness; as in *The Killdeer* this necessitates the finding of a spiritual source. "All our life," says Kingbird to one of them, "we seek our real parents, / Those who can beget and bear our souls." There is the boy-musician and -poet, Andrew Kingbird; also his sister Susan, devoted, loving, and, by virtue of her greater intellectual development, not susceptible to the enchantments of Mrs. Shade. There is Ellen Moody, locked up by a repressive mother because she is in love with Frank Fall. Frank's mother, Mrs. Fall (allegorically named), is the female counterpart of Kingbird, an intellectual woman and a piano-teacher who, although "fallen" in terms of the reigning conventions of Millbank, wants to liberate rather than to enslave the young. With Mrs. Shade come two young men, figures of impotence and vengeance because of the dark deeds of their enchantress. One of them, Stephen, tells Mrs. Shade, "Whenever I've had enough courage to look into your eyes I've seen the bottom there—of all things."

The conflict between the two principals rages throughout a Friday evening, a Saturday, and a Sunday morning. Although the comedy ends with Kingbird's congregation chastened and somewhat enlightened and with the young lovers all happily disposed of, in one sense the Manichean dualism suggested in the title is maintained; the kingdoms of darkness and light separate, with their leaders presumably going on to perform more deeds of creation or destruction. So far as Millbank is concerned, however, Mrs. Shade's very existence is now in doubt. She has been a shadowy specter from Kingbird's past, and like all shadows has disappeared when the light of truth began to shine directly above her.

III   The Easter Egg

The basic structure of *The Easter Egg* is the same as that of *The Sun and the Moon,* a conflict between enlightenment, symbolized by the sun, and tyranny and ignorance, symbolized by the shadows in which Bethel (the counterpart of Madam Fay and Mrs. Shade) would keep her victim Kenneth. Kenneth's escape from being "an attic child" is associated with entry into a green pastoral world of innocence where God is revealed. At the end, the clock which ticks towards inevitable death in most of Reaney's writings, is at least momentarily defeated by Kenneth's new awareness of himself and the world. When— through the help of substitute parents who love him, to the sound of piano music and through instruction in the art of words—Kenneth is able to shake off his traumatized childhood and its games, he leaves forever the house of his captivity. It is in the house of the sadistic stepmother Bethel, whose name, ironically, in Hebrew means "house of God," that Kenneth does break through to manhood.

In each of the three comedies just discussed the human figures moving towards the new order of reality at the end do so through a technique of finding images appropriate to their condition at each given point. This involves exploration of a mental world below the surface of consciousness and the breaking free of the traumata caused by some horrific childhood experience. In *The Killdeer,* when we first see Eli, he is impotent emotionally, intellectually, and physically; he carries a bunny and clings to his toys. His mother is, in his mind, a hawk who has shut off into a "tower of air / And a grass of fear" all posibility of her son's maturity. These images must be adapted and changed. In Harry's formulation, Eli is a hooded falcon (the hood is Eli's mother and the night world he inhabits) and Harry is the falconer who removes the hood so that Eli can mount in the tower of air to his "proper ground," the sky. The making possible of this rebirth involves the finding of new parents who in love teach a symbolic language adequate to the task. The rescues of Kenneth and Andrew in the other two comedies are similar.

It is not only the youthful protagonist who discovers himself through a metamorphosis of images; each character is so defined. It is this theatrical technique above all else which gives to Reaney's plays their peculiar beauty and power. It can be seen working more simply in his opera librettos, where the librettist's duty of writing something which the music can extend and complete leads to a paring away of complex imagery and a concentration on a few strong symbolic patterns. The technique can be seen even more simply in *One-man Masque,* a series of stage images arranged in a symbolic circle of life and death.

IV   Night-blooming Cereus

The opera *Night-blooming Cereus* is unashamedly romantic. It emerges from the same place in the author's imagination as *Twelve Letters to a Small Town* and its music is done by the same composer, John Beckwith, surely one of the happiest collaborations in the history of the arts in Canada. The libretto is subtle and sophisticated in execution, but its impact is simple and direct. Beckwith's music takes its dramatic suggestions from the words and is witty or serious, or simply commentative decoration, as required. Two chattering ninnies, girls met by the visitor who comes to the little town of Shakespeare looking for a Mrs. Brown, are musically depicted by means of a waltz tempo which disintegrates into something less secure as their conversation becomes more pointless and inane. The rhythmic and melodic threads are groping, mocking, active, melancholy, and triumphant in turn. There is spare, stringent music and there are several folk-hymn tunes which do much to establish the pastoral, small-town locale.

The theme of *Night-blooming Cereus* is human frustration and loneliness, appropriately symbolized by the cereus, whose flower appears only once in a century (actually a cereus blossoms much oftener but the romance requires a rare event). The time of the action is a Saturday night in late March and the setting is the village of Shakespeare, Ontario. Old Mrs. Brown, the protagonist, is described as one who "could easily take care of granaries" or "plant and harvest a whole farmful of crops," but who has to be content with the window-sill of a two-room cottage and "no harvest except a heart and mind filled with the delight of watching and waiting." The great disappointment of her life is that years ago her only daughter ran away to get married and never returned. As we see her at her simple household tasks—eating, washing up, sweeping, rocking, sewing, and singing a hymn at her little harmonium—the theme of loneliness is given strong expression. In the beautiful rocking chair aria there is not a false note to mar the genuine pathos of the old widow longing for the girl who "walks about beneath the sun" unconnected to her in any way.

The simple plot, developed in three scenes, brings about the union of Mrs. Brown with her daughter's daughter, Alice, come to ask of the old woman forgiveness for the long-lost girl who has recently died. Before this union takes place, however, a good deal of what the librettist has called "interior mental event"[6] transpires and four other people have become involved; they are the old woman's guests, invited to witness the opening of the cereus. As they wait, still unintroduced to Alice, whom Mrs. Brown thinks a ghost, each reveals something fundamental about himself or herself.

Reaney has explained why he chose four characters to surround Mrs. Brown and her flower:

> There is a rule in literature which says that to any tea party, or gathering of any sort, the Four Living Creatures of Ezekiel's vision attend. Actually at this time one of the few sentences of literary symbolism that had sunk through to me was Carl Jung's division of the human soul into four parts represented by an old woman, an old man, a young man and a young girl. The old woman is shadowy and terrifying, the old man is wise and helpful; the young man seeks the young woman but cannot find her until he has come to terms with the older pair.[7]

Setting aside questions of literary or psychological accuracy, we can see here the kind of psychic processes Reaney means to describe. The four characters in his opera are Mrs. Wool, the local switchboard operator, Ben, the storekeeper's son, Barbara Croft, the village orphan, and a Mr. Orchard. This fourth and last arrival, unlike the others, is spiritually integrated and strong, and also somewhat mysterious. It is he who prepares the others for the miracle which takes place at the end. On the representational level, Mr. Orchard is a gardener and neighbor, but he quickly takes on connotations of a fertility spirit as he hands out packets of seeds from his plantation up at Sunfish Lake. As described by the librettist, he "knows the mysteries of the writing in the hand, the fire in the branch, the dark lake in the head, the Saviour in the thigh."

As the group drink tea together, the roaring of a midnight train shatters their conversation and then passes into the distance. The Connecticut clock signals the beginning of Sunday. At this point the mechanical tick-tocking world of actuality and human frustration is mysteriously left behind and the little community in the cottage experience a moment of revelation:

> The clock stopped striking. Beside it stood a huge book, Mrs. Brown's Bible. It too was a sort of stove, a harmonium, a clock and a thunderous train and in it the whole world burned and did not, spoke and did not.

A hymn is sung ("Oh sweet bird sing now / Of my soul's new spring"), Mrs. Brown and Alice are quickly united, and the flower begins to open, each member of the group seeing in it what he or she desires most—a father and mother, a blacksmith's shop, nothing but a flower opening, the meaning of working in the earth, happiness and joy. The structure of auditory and visual images is completed by the singing of a chorale: "When I behold / All this glory / Then I am bold / To cross Jordan . . . / To call on God . . . / To end my story." This is the rebirth of the human soul held out in vain to Branwell by Effie. It is also the condition of light arrived at by Eli, Andrew, and Kenneth in the pastoral comedies.

V One-man Masque

The companion piece to *Night-blooming Cereus, One-man Masque,* takes a different route to the same revelation. Because it was originally played alongside *Night-blooming Cereus* and also since it too is in a limited sense a comedy, although a very dark one, it is included here. Many of its immediate affinities, however, are with the dance-of-death poems of Reaney's satirical mythos described in Chapter Two. The *Masque* represents a nightmare vision, an anatomy of human corruption. It is the climax to date of Reaney's art of the macabre, begun in early pieces like "Clay Hole" and "The Box Social," and now come to the theater in a concentrated series of sixteen grimly ironic monologues composed of images of horror and ugliness. The aim is said to be a definition of human life. A single actor moves about the stage through a motley array of props, the main ones being a cradle and a coffin, and as he goes he recites the verbal substance of the drama. Each poem rewards close attention to the subtlety and complexity of its metaphorical images. As a stage work the *Masque* makes no small demand on its listening audience's capacity to respond to a poetry much more densely wrought than anything in *Night-blooming Cereus.* The central symbolism reaches out into the whole Reaney corpus and beyond.

"The Baby" is a fifteen-stanza poem in a question-and-answer format, the first and last stanzas spoken by the narrator, the intervening ones by the baby. The baby is to tell what he built while he sat in his mother's cave, this leading to a story in two parts, accounts of violent struggle against fierce enemies

[142]

in the womb and of raging entry into the world. It is clear that the baby is generic Man as he pounds the darkness into guts, heart, and head and leads America, Eurasia, and Africa out of chaos. He is given two "boneless wands or swords," which he later recognizes as "the vorpal phallus" and "the magic tongue," from which come, respectively, biological life and human civilization. The seeds in the generative organs are the teeming animal and human life of all history, a "jostling army" showing itself in henhouse and palace, street crowds and history. The magic tongue is "Stuffed with names and numbers, / The string of song," and symbolizes in Blakean fashion the great human constructs of the verbal and numerical universes by which civilized man wakes himself "from fallen slumbers." Once born, the furious baby rages, "An old man one hour old," a bridegroom come to his world-bride who is "Careless, unready and cold." He at birth is a seed again, left to make his way in a vast cave towards the "sun-egg" which is his destiny "steeples far away." The imagery is complex but the Blakean idea is simple: human desire and physical nature are antithetical so that the former, to avoid defeat, must use all the resources of body, heart, and mind to conquer the latter.

Other forms emerge in this odyssey of definition. The narrator tells a child who as just learned to walk that he can walk only as well as he can talk, the "Alphabet" theme, and then proceeds to teach him a grammar lesson. Adolescence is seen through the distorting perspective of the principal of a private boys' academy whose interest in the boys is not at all academic and whose perverse delight in playing havoc with youthful lives rivals that of Madam Fay or Bethel. "Rachel" tells of a golden foundling child taken in and loved by the poet, only to become in his absence from her a cosmeticized freak living the life of an expensive prostitute. Rachel is destroyed in the name of virtue and thrown like Jezebel from her balcony, leaving a baby over whom the poet in the manner of Amos laments, "My darling, it is my fault— / I have not tears enough." The mythical contours of the poem are made clear, through reference to Christ, Jezebel, the Scarlet Lady, and a dragon. The biblical theme of divine *caritas*, however, is reversed, and harlotry wins over redeeming love.

"The Telephone" involves a conversation between a middle-aged man and someone called Eric. This is a lively satire on complacent self-absorption in the presence of acute human need. Eric is about to have a nervous breakdown but is provided with a long list of reasons why the speaker cannot meet with him this week, or next week, or any other week, until, perhaps, after the Judgment and the Second Coming.

"Doomsday," a hortatory, exuberant, and gruesome invocation of the world's dead to spring their coffin lids for the resurrection parties and balls, is followed by "The Dwarf," the most malevolent of all the figures in this study of the human form. He catalogs his achievements: sold by his father, he became a court jester, and his jests, in their cruelty, have far outdone the jests of Lear's Fool. He has turned the young queen mad with lust, created a Cain-Abel situation between the princes, destroyed the servants' faith in angels, degraded the swineherd, frustrated the elopement of the princess, and filled the court with lust. He has even set the four elements at war with each other and, as a final annihilation of all created harmonies, he has had the the minstrel's tongue cut off. Now the castle is empty, inside out, and he lives alone among the ruins, "the compressed cause of everything." He crawls into a manger, props up the dead queen's body, and calls for some shepherds to adore:

> To the curious observant baby
> The humble and the royal bow
> Hush a bye my baby do, for see
> That spider on your mother's brow.

If from one critical perspective literary irony is parodied myth, it is easy to see that "The Dwarf" is a parody of myths of creation, redemption, and incarnation.

If *One-man Masque* ended there, in a parody of divine love, one might conclude that its sole purpose was to shock. But Reaney is writing satire and this means that in some way his aim is moral, redemptive, as is the case with all serious satire. To take apart a rotting body is the work of a ghoul, unless some rational principle is operating. The *Masque* ends with a poem called "The Lost Child" in which Milton's Holy Ghost bird searches in a wintry, moribund world and over an empty sea for a lost human life. He finds the cradle beside the coffin, rescues it, and in the posture of a shepherd kneels beside it, saying,

> I push the shore and kingdom to you,
> O winter walk with seed pod ditch:
> I touch them to the floating child
> And lo! Cities and gardens, shepherds and smiths.

Satire makes its moral norms clear. Here it is a matter of creative work and civilization set against perversity and destruction. In the image of the cradle rescued from the coffin to become Christ's birthplace, we see that *One-man Masque* arrives at the same destination as *Night-blooming Cereus* and the other comedies, even though the road there has fewer flashes of human glory to light the way.

VI   The Shivaree

The Shivaree, whose music is now being composed by John Beckwith, is an opera libretto in two acts. Like *Night-blooming Cereus* it takes its design from an abstract mythical pattern and is structurally a romantic comedy. It is a burlesque of the story of Eurydice (or Persephone) and her descent into, and escape from, Hades. The elegiac seriousness of the earlier opera is replaced by a mood of high jinks and whoop-de-doo reminiscent of the American ballet *Rodeo*. In addition to its mythological source, *The Shivaree* reaches into folk culture in rural Canada. A "shivaree" (the French *charivari*) is a raucous serenade in the middle of the night for a bride and groom, on the wedding night itself, if the couple can be found, or immediately after their return from the honeymoon. The participants are the unmarried men of the community and the aim is to keep the groom from enjoying his bride until he has paid a price in money, beer, or whiskey. The money is sometimes used to buy liquid refreshment, sometimes to pay for an orchestra for a community dance; there is no mention of the second in Reaney's libretto. The ritual normally involves only good-natured bawdry and a kind of tin-kettle sanctioning of the marriage. If, however, the bridegroom is unpopular or unaccommodating, rougher actions may take place. The prudent groom gives quickly and generously.

The Shivaree is set about 1900 in a rural Canadian community. It concerns a marriage which should never have taken place and which must therefore not be allowed to be consummated. The bridegroom is anything but young, handsome, and loving. His name is Mr. Quartz and he has previously had two wives who have died simply from being Mrs. Quartz. He is wealthy and avaricious, his home (a farmhouse which is a country store) being variously described as a Mammon's cave or as filled with clouds, rain, dead leaves, and snow. He is associated with spiders and with a prize possession, a black stallion called Cerberus. In his house also lives his spinster sister Henrietta, "a formidable bird of a woman," whose delight is in keeping accounts and fondling cash-boxes.

As the action begins we see the Persephone figure, a pretty girl called Daisy, being taken home from her wedding by Mr. Quartz in a buggy drawn by Cerberus. This, in line with the abstract design, involves passage through a swamp and forest which blot out the sun. Daisy has just now wakened up to the fact that her only reason for agreeing to marry was to make jealous the shy and indecisive young man she really loves, Jonathan. More ludicrous than pathetic, she refuses to get down out of the buggy and proceeds, rather dim-wittedly, to take stock of her situation. Her new husband does not help matters in his admission that he does not love her, although he is lustful enough, nor in his insistence that, although he cannot remember her name, his many possessions should make her happy. The recalcitrant Jonathan, described by Quartz as a young capon and by the librettist as an elegant Orpheus, arrives on the scene in time to sing an unhappy duet and share a sunset with Daisy, after which she sadly goes into Mr. Quartz's house, resigned to her misalliance.

Meanwhile a counter-action has begun, involving Jonathan, the shivaree band, and a Miss Beech. This last is a gentle old schoolteacher who goes "botanizing" down the country roads on her bicycle and, in accord with her function as a latter day Ceres, has determined that Daisy will get away from her Pluto. Act II, beginning with a description of the lunar beauties of a perfect midsummer wedding night, shows us the shivaree and the resultant rescue of Daisy for Jonathan, all accompanied by an intermittent associating of the action with the ancient fertility myth which structures the text. Also, there is a delightfully arbitrary twist of the plot to get round the difficulty of Daisy already being Mrs. Quartz, plus a second quite unexpected marriage. *The Shivaree* is a lively, witty entertainment, a kind of spoof, among other things, on the poet's own myth-opeic tendencies.

VII *The Plays for Children*

It is perhaps in Reaney's theatrical work for children that one can see his basic dramatic intentions most clearly. He wants to fashion plays with the help of the child or the adult's imagination itself, and to do so he exploits patterns of human life and experience which are sensational, simplified, and, in their way, deadly accurate. The sensationalism is simply a controlled means to a particular end, a way of exploding drearier ways of looking at things, so that a kind of psychological accuracy becomes possible. The theater-goer too sophisticated to let melodramatic art have its place will not get far with any Reaney play, for each one uses the two main themes of melodrama, the triumph of spiritual goodness over villainy and the idealizing of the sense of what is acceptable and right assumed to be held by the audience. Still, if that were all, one could safely dismiss these plays as only for the childish and simple-minded. What saves them from naïveté and triviality is their exuberant sense of verbal sport, their highly controlled use of well-proven fictional formulas, and the poetic richness of their conceptions.

Reaney's marionette plays, *Little Red Riding Hood* and *Apple Butter,* were both adapted from simple folklore stories with a built-in appeal for the young, as the enthusiastic response of hundreds of children has shown. The marionettes for *Apple Butter* were created from simple geometrical forms (circles, squares, half circles) by the artist Greg Curnoe, and given an equally abstract setting by Jack Chambers. By this very obvious subtraction from reality, coupled with the peculiar animation possible with marionettes, the child's fancy is made to work and the simple emotional contours of a story about an innocent little girl threatened by a wicked wolf are reconstructed by the child himself.

Names and Nicknames, a play for children directed at the Manitoba Theatre Centre by John Hirsch and Robert Sherrin in 1963, is a simplified version of several important elements in Reaney's writings. There is the basic situation of innocent children flanked by both malign and malevolent adult figures. The setting is an Ontario farm in the 'thirties (it is also that of "the Farmer in the Dell" in the nursery rhyme) and there is a good deal of attention given to the changing seasons, the times of the day, and the various farm tasks associated with these rhythms of nature. There is even a sub-plot in which the hired man Rob, who at eighteen has not yet tried his high school entrance examination, is trying to marry the better educated and pretty Etta. Farmer Dell and his wife have a series of three babies during the years of the play's action but are prevented from having them properly christened by the hostility of Old Grandpa Thorntree, who gives insulting nicknames to all children born in the community. Thorntree has his antithesis in the wise and loving clergyman, the Reverend Hackaberry, who is a simplified version of Kingbird in *The Sun and the Moon.* Everything is finally worked out satisfactorily and the play ends with a party which is both a christening and a wedding celebration. The means of resolution is an exorcism of hatred through learning enough words to vanquish the enemy, the same theme explored in more depth in *The Easter Egg.*

VIII   Listen to the Wind

As a stage production *Names and Nicknames* can be seen as an experiment leading directly to the recent play *Listen to the Wind.* Hirsch used only six trained actors, plus a group of children and the audience itself. Aside from a few simple props and some rhythm band instruments, the play depended on mime and words, the latter pared to an extreme simplicity and culled from an old *Practical Speller* owned by the playwright's father. Reaney's conception of the kind of theatrical art involved in these two plays is indicated in his program notes for *Listen to*

the Wind: "Art is made by substracting from reality & letting
the viewer imagine or 'dream it out.' . . ." He connects the
simple style of his play with a scene of mime and gestures in
a centuries-old drama, *At the Fairy Mountain Bridge,* produced
by the Peking National Opera.

Despite its length, its unusual demands on an audience, and
its effective alienation of some spectators, the production of
Listen to the Wind was one of the most gripping and imagina-
tively effective amateur theatricals in the history of Canadian
theater. It is difficult to see, although not everyone agrees,
how a professional rendition could do anything other than im-
pair its freshness and spontaneity and its deft ways of involving
a majority of the audience in the work of creation.[8] Chief
among the last of these was a Chorus of fourteen children,
dressed in their own casual summer clothes and serving a
variety of purposes. Like the orchestra of the Peking Opera
they sit at stage-left, where, when they are not directly for-
warding the action by providing props or characters or sound-
effects, they serve as audience for the play within the play,
"The Saga of Caresfoot Court," which makes up the bulk of
the drama. By simple mimesis they become a forest thicket,
guests at a garden party, lilies in a garden, servants at a ban-
quet, a collection of starving dogs, and a flock of birds shot
at by the play's villain. One child becomes a stag. Another,
a little girl with black hair and white face, plays a baby ghost,
while a small blonde is a fierce mastiff, agent of the cruel
squire's nemesis. The Chorus play instruments, sing, click stones
for the sound of an oven bird, and make cricket noises with
combs.

Although it follows the conventional division into three acts,
Listen to the Wind is structurally unusual. There are forty-nine
scenes, which points up the complete unimportance in the play
of elaborate trappings or any adherence to rigid categories of
time and space. In the outer play the setting is a Perth County,
Ontario, farmhouse in the 'thirties. Here four children, a boy
Owen and his three cousins, Harriet, Jenny, and Ann, gather
for a summer and entertain themselves by acting out plays,
drawing when necessary on the help of several adults and other
neighborhood children. This action is both light-hearted and

pathetic, for underneath the playing lies the fact of Owen's lingering sickness, which seems certain to end in his death, and also the desertion of his father by his mother; without maternal love Owen's situation is desperate and his play-acting is an attempt to draw his mother back from her lover on the neighboring farm. Owen's father, Mr. Taylor, is weak and ineffective, more enraged that his wife has taken a prized horse than that she has abandoned her family.

In the families of Harriet and Ann there are lesser tragedies, although these are only mentioned. The suggestion is that the movement into theatrical creation is an attempt to impose a more brilliantly colored and strongly drawn pattern on the dreary, frustrating actualities in the children's lives. The play's offering of alternative endings for the inner drama, one tragic and the other comic, is a way of saying that it is the prerogative of the liberated imagination to improve on the ravages of nature. But the facts of nature are still there, as the story of Owen reminds us, and although we cannot tell for sure whether he is to die or not, at least it is clear that his mother has finally gone, his father is still ineffectual, and no substitute parents have been found to nourish him towards maturity, as in the case of Eli in *The Killdeer* or Kenneth in *The Easter Egg*.

Actions in the outer play merge almost imperceptibly into those of the inner play, "The Saga of Caresfoot Court." This is a Victorian melodramatic novel, based closely but in an abbreviated way on H. Ryder Haggard's early novel *Dawn*. In this story a beautiful heroine threads "her way through a world of evil manorhouses and sinister Lady Eldreds," in an action analogous to Owen's struggle. The novel was Owen's father's gift to Mrs. Taylor just before they married. In this inner story the fictional characters are drawn in thick black pencil. Their relations are diagrammatically conceived; sharp antitheses of good and bad, strong and weak, beautiful and ugly are unmistakable. Owen's story runs a summer only; the Caresfoot narrative spans two generations, about twenty years.

The settings of "The Saga" vary. In the main they are three Victorian country houses, Caresfoot Court, Hawkscliffe Hall, and the Grange, but there are also outdoor scenes in the woods, by the streams, and in the nearby village of Roxham. There are also brief scenes on the Island of Madeira, at an inn in the Alps, and on a ship approaching England. Caresfoot Court reaches back into history for its associations, having come into the Caresfoot family in the time of Henry VIII's spoliation of the monasteries, and has become legendary in the region by virtue of Caresfoot's Staff, an ancient oak planted by the original Caresfoot when he was a swineherd in need of a staff. This staff now symbolizes the family tree and branches.

Hawkscliffe Hall is a larger estate on which the young, plain gentlewoman Maria Lawry, who plays the role of betrayed maiden, lives. The Grange is the house from which evil reaches out to destroy all possibility of happiness in the other two houses. Madeira, suggested by a potted palm and a song based on a poem by Emily Brontë about a South Sea paradise called Ula's bower, is the place of exile for Angela's fiancé Arthur Brenzaida. In her darkest hour Angela longs to see the wild swans on the Caresfoot estate lake, but they have not yet made their seasonal return; Arthur, slowly proceeding across Europe towards her, sees the swans on a lake by an Alpine inn.

The story centers round Angela, the beautiful but despised daughter of the mercenary Piers Caresfoot, who, through contravening his aged father's wishes and marrying someone else, has at his father's death been disinherited, in favor of the repulsive, adoptive son, the "cowbird" Douglas. Angela, whose mother died giving birth to her, is unwillingly made her father's chief instrument in his attempt to regain his former possessions. Not until late in the story does she realize his full malignity. Although she loves Arthur, she is persuaded that he is dead and so, filled with loathing, accedes to her father's wish to marry Douglas.

Years before, Douglas joined forces with the witch-lady Geraldine Almeda and she, through an opportune marriage, has become the malevolent but beautiful Lady Eldred. She is the inner play's counterpart to the cruel mother of Owen and has begun her rise from gipsydom to lady by killing her baby fathered by Douglas. Like Madam Fay, Bethel, and Charlotte Shade, only more so, Lady Eldred is an infernal character associated with sorcery and the black arts. Like all Reaney's fully drawn characters, she is portrayed through images; she is a wolf in the forest catching deer by the throat, a "hell dog," a creature of weasel's nests and crooked heart. When her witch-craft is finally defeated, she sits paralyzed in a wheel-chair, staring "at a certain evil winking star." Her name "Eldred" presumably means "fear of God," or perhaps "scourge of God," in keeping with her symbolic function of antithesis to the "heavenly messenger," Angela. Although her hatred of the in-habitants of Caresfoot Court is explained by cruelty long ago by the dead squire to her gipsy father, she is primarily the playwright's plot engineer. When her dramatic work is done, she sinks into listlessness and unimportance.

The influence of the Brontës on Reaney's play is pronounced. Like the four Brontë children who survived childhood—Bran-well, Charlotte, Emily, and Ann—Reaney's boy and three girls are isolated, deprived of adequate parental love, and gifted with extraordinary powers of fancy. Like the Bontës, Owen and the girls get help in "listening to the wind" from four adults, a doctor, a housekeeper, a father, and a sexton. The last three are readily identifiable from the Brontë story. Tabby—she has the same name in Reaney's play as in Haworth parsonage—is the old Brontë servant and nurse. There is the father, always in the background helping to feed the imaginations of the children but, in his massive self-sufficiency, not really taking care of their emotional needs. And Mitch, Owen's crony who takes care of the church, is based on John Brown, the Haworth sexton, stonemason, gravedigger, and highly intelligent friend of Bran-well Brontë. Owen, at one point bellowing out Tarzan lines and at another crying for his mother's arms, is Branwell Brontë in his dual role as a Gondal character who lives hard, loves des-perately, and dies cursing, but who cannot make real life meas-ure up to his fantasies.

The title of Reaney's play, aparently comes, whether con-sciously or not, from a Branwell Brontë letter.[9] Wind and storm motifs run through the Brontë letters, poems, and novels as an accompaniment to human emotions. Close examination of the lines of *Listen to the Wind* reveals how pervasive the Brontë influence is: in the poems of Charlotte and Emily that become a substantial part of the Chorus's utterances, in the large sym-bolism, in the choice of names from the Angrian and Gondal romances, and in lesser ways. Owen, for example, talks about his "nerves," recalling Branwell Brontë's exclamation one evening when he had escaped Haworth parsonage to go with a friend to ride in a rocking boat in the town: "Oh! my nerves! my nerves! Oh my nerves!" Or to take another random example —at one point in her isolated girlhood Angela asks the clergyman Mr. Gleneden, "What lies over there behind these hills. Beyond the forest. Is it the sea?" Almost the same words are used by Cathy Linton in *Wuthering Heights* when, at thirteen, she questions Nelly Dean about the world outside the Grange.

In its symbolic patterning *Listen to the Wind* is lifted from the level of naive fiction to a penetrating study of the workings of the creative imagination. Jay Macpherson describes it this way: "'Listening to the wind' is the play's image for openness to imagination: the willingness to listen is that willed passiveness in which the Spirit can move." Early in Act I we are alerted to the central meaning: "Once there were four children who listened to the wind."

The North Wind announces the malign influences of Lady Eldred and Douglas, a "fierce howling mother with the rain her doll" and a "black huntsman and his men." As with Mr. Lockwood, the observer-narrator in *Wuthering Heights*, on the stormy night he stays in Heathcliff's house and is absorbed into its dark mysteries, so here the North Wind writes on the frosty pane and scratches on the listener's "crystal brain." Atmospheric tumult, "wuthering" forces, lull the dreamer "awake. Keen keen awake."

The South Wind, the thaw wind, symbolizes the happy but brief and precarious spring and summer in which the love of Piers and Claudia blossoms and bears fruit. The Night Wind clears clouds away from the moon's face. It is linked with the long-lived affection of Owen and Harriet for each other and, since they play these parts in the Caresfoot story, with that of Arthur and Angela as well. Harriet says of this wind: "The wind we listen to—blows white sails to Eternity." The East Wind shares certain meanings with the North Wind. It is bitterly cold and malevolent and is identified with the malice and the concerted will of Lady Eldred, Douglas, and Piers; it sweeps Angela like a dead leaf towards a repugnant marriage, which

culminates in her madness and, in one of the inner play's endings, her death. When Douglas comes to Caresfoot Court on
his wedding night to claim his victim-bride, it is the East Wind
that blows down the ancestral Staff. The West Wind is a messenger of hope and liberty, invoked by Angela to free her from
the winter of her imprisonment to Lady Eldred's sorcery. She
goes to Arthur Brenzaida's ball on a horse called "The West
Wind," riding through a snow-covered moonlit forest, where
wild stags flit past. The wind symbolism of the play indicates
that, at its structural base, *Listen to the Wind* is another of
Reaney's reworkings of the story of the victory of spring over
winter. Even at the nadir of the action, in a piece called "The
Storm Poem," there is mention of a last sheaf left in the fields
for the evil huntsman as a *Golden Bough* token of the inevitable
resurgence of life.

Integrated with the symbolism of the winds in a pattern of
demonic versus benevolent forces, there is a wealth of imagery.
The nightmare descent into "the world below" uncovers a malignant doll enclosing the wishbone of a murdered baby, mad
dogs, owls, spiders, the horse hooves of the Goblin of death,
a tooth from Medusa's head, and a false funeral at midnight.
But there are also images of joy—violin music, a lovers' ring, a
star of love in a deep blue evening sky, and four genii described
as presiding over the eternal forms of Owen, Harriet, Jenny,
and Ann.

Listen to the Wind is a theatrical *tour-de-force* capable of
standing on its own special qualities. To read the script is to
have only the palest reflection of the play as play; it is not the
fascinating reading experience that *The Killdeer* is. Still, it is
worthy of study, partly as a synthesis of much that Reaney has
written to date. It displays his uncanny knowledge of the minds
and emotions of imaginative children, his life-long fascination
with the macabre and with perennial patterns of romance. It
also displays as well as anything he has written his capacity
to create a verbal world which has its own color and music,
its own peculiar way of winning an esthetic triumph over those
things which bedevil the life of the imaginative innocent. Perhaps not least of all, there is the vital connection between
Listen to the Wind and the fantasies "dreamed out" thirty years
ago in a lonely Gothic farmhouse near Stratford.

[154]

CHAPTER 4

Reaneyland: Conclusion

IT has been suggested in several places in this book that James
Reaney has a claim to consideration as a major poet and
that this is at least partly because his individual works add up
to a total imaginative construct, Reaneyland, which is larger
and more significant than any single one or group of them.
In *The Red Heart* poems and in the other juvenilia there is a
pronounced sense of imaginative energy looking for somewhere
to go and for a means of going there. The nihilistic absorption
with death and silence as the end of all endeavors is a consequence of the failure at that time to find a way. The original
energy is still at work, but from the time of compositions like
Night-blooming Cereus and *A Suit of Nettles* in the mid-fifties,
Reaney has been busy at work consciously constructing his own
peculiar myth of the rebirth of the human soul or, in the communal terms underlying his magazine *Alphabet*, of the building
of Jerusalem's wall in Canada's vast and not so pleasant land.
So far as his own writings are concerned, this missionary activity involves use of what he calls a "symbolic grammar" or
"literary geometry," a language of iconography learned from
the Bible, Spenser, Shakespeare, Blake, Yeats, and Northrop
Frye.[1] The result is not the kind of barren transplanting of for-
eign traditions into Canada that marred so much of her early
literature. Rather, and this is a tribute both to Reaney's powers
and to the archetypal "aliveness" of the tradition he has
espoused, the result has been the creation of some of the best
writing Canada has ever produced. On the surface Reaneyland
is wayward, macabre, even perverse at times, but the more it
is examined the more it can be seen as part of an ancestral
wisdom.

Reaneyland is a state of mind in which you are asked to see
things in a new way, an idealized, simplified way. As in Blake

and Yeats, large antitheses prevail in the handling of human figures; kingdoms of darkness and light are locked in violent conflict and human life emerges as caught up in a kind of cataclysm or fundamental anatomizing out of which new insight and maturity are meant to emerge. The imaginative world in which this takes place (and quite a few Reaney critics have apparently not seen this) has only an oblique, albeit a very important, connection with the world of ordinary, waking reality. The state of mind necessary for the protagonist is the one in which he comes to see clearly all the things he fears and all the things he loves in sharp conflict. The reader or audience is invited to leave behind ordinary logical thought processes and enter into works of art symbolizing spiritual metamorphoses.

The initiate in a Reaney tale has to learn to play at some of the horrifying things real people do to each other. He has to go through a cyclical funhouse—each Reaney play *is* this—in order to learn what it is to become a completed self. The funhouse is located in an imagined mental landscape, conceived in moral terms, into which eternity is forcing its way with the purpose of revealing infernal powers as finally impotent in terms of a higher reality, and by this revelation inducing a purgatorial ascent. Reaneyland is not the real world and it is not heaven; it is that condition in which an awareness of heaven makes possible the beginnings of the reconstruction of the so-called real world.

In an article already cited, Reaney talks of Carl Jung's division of the soul into four parts, represented by an old woman, an old man, a young man, and a young girl. The younger two cannot come together until the young man has come to terms with the older pair. When this has happened, however, a new human soul is integrated or born. It is not difficult to see that, although Reaney's comment was made about *Night-blooming Cereus* and the preparation of Mrs. Conrad Brown for the rebirth of her soul, it underlies the patterning of character in his other fictions. In *The Killdeer*, Eli is reborn through the workings of his "terrible mother" Madam Fay, the "wise old man" Dr. Ballad, the young man Harry (the *animus*), and the young woman Rebecca (the *anima*). Harry becomes capable of serving a redemptive purpose because earlier he has torn himself free

[156]

from his mother and the vulture-wife Vernelle. In confrontation with Mr. Manatee, Harry is mature enough to win on the only level that matters, although he loses in terms of physical strength. Unknown to him, his wise old man or guardian is mysteriously working in the background while in the foreground action his *anima*, Rebecca, becomes his wife. Reaney underlines the symbolism of *The Killdeer* by having an actual baby, a new soul, born to receive Eli's toys.

The other works are simpler but also use the four-part pattern. In *The Sun and the Moon* Andrew Kingbird is located between the polarities of his wise father and Charlotte Shade, and between the *anima* Susan and the *animus* Frank Fall. Stephen and Dennis are demonic, shadowy anti-souls. In *The Easter Egg* the terrible mother (stepmother) is Bethel Henry, the wise counselor is Dr. Ira Hill, the benevolent female figure is Polly, and the young man is George, whose sadism has to be conquered by the reborn Kenneth. In *The Shivaree* a proper epithalamium cannot be sung for Jonathan and Daisy before the workings of Henrietta and Mr. Quartz are cancelled out. There is no wise old man here, appropriately enough, since the opera works on a very light-hearted level. *Listen to the Wind*, spanning as it does two generations and involving both an inner and an outer story, has more variants in its symbolism. There are two cruel mother figures, Mrs. Taylor and Lady Eldred, played by the same actress. Taken all together, Mr. Taylor, Dr. Spettigue, and Mr. Gleneden might conceivably add up to one wise old man. Owen, in the outer story, has his Harriet and, in the inner story, Arthur finally is united with his Angela. Throughout the play Owen's struggle to find a love that will usher him into manhood is reflected by the ghost of Lady Eldred's baby, which appears from time to time looking for its true mother; only when Angela, years later, can kiss the malignant doll does the ghost rest easy.

Reaney is a writer given to the use of old-fashioned words like "heart" and "soul," which does not always go down well with the more "sophisticated" members of his public. There is nothing particularly novel or mysterious in his ideas on these subjects. Human maturity is the result of a quest involving body, heart, and mind. The goal is a synthesis of all three. This is not easily obtainable for the children who dwell in Reaney-land, surrounded as they are by witches and other demonic beings. A great deal of the emotional tension in *The Red Heart* comes from the poet's feeling that there is a vast gulf between what he desires and what his mind tells him about reality. In *A Suit of Nettles* Branwell fails, on the whole, in his spiritual quest, because he cannot find a path between his head and his body. Mopsus, however, through the instructions of Effie, is able to accept the lord who "is most like a sun for he / Makes his beholders into suns, / Shadowless and timeless." A similar progress is described in each of Reaney's later works.

The obstacles to growth are numerous. There is the kind of entanglement in emotion and passion which cripples Branwell and there is the self-centeredness shown by Jonathan in Act I of *The Shivaree*. Mopsus' early rejection of the world of nature in favor of an abstraction is equally inadequate, in terms of a final desired synthesis. Eli, Kenneth, and Owen all have been afflicted from childhood by trauma-inducing adult brutality and neglect, so that the main characteristic of each is a fear of leaving childhood. Even in the fetal state, the baby in *One-man Masque* has to battle against tyrannous nature. Reaney's most exuberant symbol for dictatorial and destructive forces pitted against child victims is the dragon lady or witch who possesses her victim and tempts him into death's kingdom. Her accomplices are her sinister male lovers, weaker figures who take what strength they have from their association with the enchantress. In only one Reaney work, *The Killdeer*, are there destroying male figures, Mr. Manatee and Clifford, who rival in strength the terrible mother figure. In two works, *One-man Masque* and *The Sun and the Moon*, a dwarf figure appears, to help "phenomenologize" the journey from death to life; in the latter, the Tramp, who looks like a dwarf, is an agent of Mrs. Shade.

More than one woman reader or theater-goer has complained about Reaney's depictions of the self-effacing female figure who is the antithesis to the witch. The assumption usually appears to be that these and the other human figures in a Reaney text are meant to be psychologically "rounded." They are not. Effie, Rebecca, Susan, Polly, and Angela are all stylized redemptrix figures, several of them explicitly linked with Christ. If one is proceeding on a psychological plane, it sounds like monstrous uxoriousness when Harry calls Rebecca "the source" of all goodness and creativity, and Effie can be seen as having too much of "Hohum Humble" in her makeup. But reading this way one can also reduce to foolishness the story of the pilgrim-soul Dante guided by Beatrice, or of Darley in *The Alexandria Quartet*, permitted to pass into an eternal kingdom through the relationship with Clea. The benevolent female in Reaney's writings is a symbol of the artist's soul, the completely unified self or guardian angel who appears at the nadir of the protagonist's experience to help him past some insuperable barrier which if it is not conquered will bring death. Reaney, like Spenser and Yeats, to name only two, makes the ideal woman a repository of wisdom and a guide who brings metaphors and images to enable the artist to progress, because, perhaps, women seem to come to a vision of certainty more readily than men do. These figures help the protagonists to trace each emotional event to its cause and turn it into usable knowledge. They perform merciful actions so selflessly that they should be able to dissolve any male's self-centeredness. Also since Reaney's is an imagination which works in antithetical symbols, the idealizing and simplifying involved here helps make possible the creation of the antithetical, violent females who precipitate the action in the heart and mind of the protagonist.

Another possible misunderstanding of Reaney's concern with the development of the artistic consciousness is to see this as a kind of late-Romantic deification of an individual artist. Reaney is more Jungian than Freudian. By this I mean that the baring of childhood traumata and the concern with the unconscious in his writings are only a step on the way to something more than the freeing of an individual psyche. They are a movement into what Jung called the collective unconscious or into what Blake found when he passed into the impersonal part of his own mind and discovered all minds. At this point, as Mopsus discovers, the individual begins to see with the eyes of God. It is here, then, that we locate the impersonal reserve and wisdom of the Reverend Mr. Kingbird or Mr. Gleneden or Dr. Ballad; they are not little egos carping and rattling but wise exemplars of understanding and charity, the central figures in the humane, civilized community which emerges at the end of the comedies.

The community thus revealed is Reaney's "kingdom of the sun," the desirable goal just beyond the uppermost limit of Reaneyland. It has taken years for Reaney to develop the symbolism of this kingdom. When first mentioned in *The Red Heart*, it is a place of escape from the "great sad real" world "filled . . . with blood, pus, horror, death, stepmothers, and lies." By the mid-fifties, however, the kingdom of the sun has been developed as a full-fledged visionary alternative to the sterile land. Destructive fantasies are the most vivid part of the Red Heart's world, but in *A Suit of Nettles* and the comedies these fantasies are shown to be the manifestations of adults who are still children taking revenge on a world which has denied them love as children. They are more; they are denizens of a hellish world of shadows, refugees from cruelty shown them earlier, now intent on claiming their own victims in turn. As Reaneyland points more and more insistently towards the kingdom of the sun, the earlier somewhat ghoulish fascination with the macabre and the destructive takes on a positive antithetical force. The desirable kingdom is no longer a hopelessly distant, beautiful place but a state within human consciousness.

Towards the conclusion of his doctoral dissertation, Reaney makes certain statements which help to explain the role he has set for himself as dramatist, in a country notoriously unproductive of, and hostile to, native playwrights. In English literary history he distinguishes two major poetic traditions, one a popular, English, Protestant, and revolutionary one, the other esoteric, French-inspired, Catholic, and conservative. His reading of Yeats leads him to the conclusion that Lady Gregory transplanted Yeats from the latter tradition to the former, to a sense of his own personal possession of the Word of God, thus drawing him from an esthete's world where he played with fragile, beautiful things out into the public arena. In Reaney's development there is something closely analogous, a decision not to be content with the creation of a private world, or even with getting at people secretly in a book, but to launch a frontal assault, as editor, university teacher, playwright, and director. He sees in poets like Spenser, Milton, Blake, and Yeats a belief in an energetic attack on the problem of man's recovering control of event and circumstance. This is not the conservative tradition represented in our time by Eliot, in which you wait for the world to come to its realization of the meaning of the hanged god while you go about your ritual observances.

James Reaney is a poet who believes in hanging up the "Images of the life that was in Eden," in reliance on an inner vision of reality which takes its source in the New Testament and is kept alive wherever faith in the creative power of the Word and the imaginative liberty emanating from it are stronger than faith in reasonable conformity to any social, political, or ecclesiastical convention. He learned as a child the bibliolatry of what he calls the "Protestant left," through the sectarian religion of the Plymouth Brethren and the Congregationalists, and he is still greatly attracted to the intensity of vision and belief in an inner light characteristic of the Quaker movement. At the same time he works with a poetic and symbolic language which antedates all his literary mentors, the language established for the Western world by early churchmen like Saint Augustine, Isidore of Seville, and the Venerable Bede, a language by which man was enabled to read the world as the second book of God, as a dictionary of types and symbols. In Reaney's reading of literary history this language was surrendered by the great Romantics, like Goethe, Wordsworth, and Browning, who espoused a literature which was primarily a criticism of life and an interpretation of things as they are in the world to which Mutability pays her attention. The other, older tradition—the one of the Anglo-Saxon scops, Chaucer, Langland, Spenser, Milton, Blake, and Yeats—is Reaney's, for in it he sees a way of getting outside nature and beyond Reaneyland into a world of realized ideals. In this land-of-heart's-desire, towards which the poetic imagination aspires, the human mind is represented as having embraced all experience, beginning, in the case of this particular poet, with the fantasies of a dreaming child in a lonely farmhouse and moving from there through the symbolic lore of a whole culture. This culture, based on the Classical and Christian mythologies, is in turn thought of as intermittently breaking through, in the achievements of its visionary artists, to the timeless, ideal pattern of itself.

Notes and References

Chapter One

1. These images and ideas are characteristic of *The Red Heart*, but are taken from the untitled poem which introduces Reaney's novel *Afternoon Moon*, only the first part of which, unfortunately, has been published. See *Here and Now*, 1 (May, 1948), 38-46.
2. See the *Literary History of Canada: Canadian Literature in English*, general editor Carl F. Klinck (Toronto: University of Toronto Press, 1965).
3. See note 1 above.
4. *Canadian Short Stories*, ed. Robert Weaver and Helen James (Toronto: Oxford University Press, 1952); also in *Canadian Short Stories*, ed. Robert Weaver ("The World's Classics" [London: Oxford University Press, 1962]).

Chapter Two

1. "The Influence of Spenser on Yeats" (unpublished Ph.D. dissertation, University of Toronto, 1958).
2. Mackenzie is a hero in Reaney's reading of Canadian history. He returns to him in his book-length story for children, *The Boy with an R in His Hand* (Toronto: Macmillan of Canada, 1965).
3. See *Collected Poems of Raymond Knister*, ed. and with memoir by Dorothy Livesay (Toronto: The Ryerson Press, 1949).
4. Its Spenserian analogue is the fable about the "goodly Oake" and the "bragging brere" in "Febrvarie"; in each story an insulting arrogant and aggressive speaker, the Briar and the Door respectively, attacks his humble opposite who is simply minding his own business. Each according to the rule of nemesis, is destroyed. Beyond this similarity of situation and theme, and the fact that both fables are told in rhyming couplets, there seems to be little dependence of Reaney's fable on Spenser's.
5. Isabella Valancy Crawford (1850-1887) was a poet, novelist, and writer of short stories who lived in Ontario from the age of eight, at Paisley, Lakefield, Peterborough, and Toronto. Her poems are notable for the power of their conception and for their fresh

use of Indian imagery. Like Reaney, she was interested in melodramatic depictions of human life and in putting poetic forms on Canadian landscapes. See *The Collected Poems of Isabella Valancy Crawford*, ed. J. W. Garvin (Toronto: Wm. Briggs, 1905). Duncan Campbell Scott (1862-1947), a poet and writer of short stories, spent much of his life in Ottawa in the Department of Indian Affairs. He is noted for his portrayals of the Canadian wilderness and of man's emotions in relation to it. See his collected works, *Poems of Duncan Campbell Scott* (Toronto: McClelland & Stewart, 1926).

6. See Lyman J. Chapman & Donald F. Putnam. *The Physiography of Southern Ontario* (Toronto: University of Toronto Press, 1951).

7. In Spenser's "June" Hobbinol recommends that Colin go to the dale where no "gastly owles doe flee." Reaney elaborates the idea considerably.

8. Northrop Frye uses the term "low mimetic" in the first part of his *Anatomy of Criticism* (Princeton: Princeton University Press, 1957) to indicate the mode of writing in which the characters display a power of action roughly that of ordinary men, as in most comedy and realistic fiction.

9. Donald Creighton, *Dominion of the North: A History of Canada* (new ed.; Toronto: Macmillan of Canada, 1957).

10. Reaney returns to the imagery of transcontinentalism in the Centennial Collage for radio done in collaboration with John Beckwith. Part One, broadcast November 23, 1965, and February 13, 1966, is entitled "Canada Dash, Canada Dot: The Line Across"; Part Two is "The Line Up and Down," not yet broadcast; a third and final part is planned for 1967.

11. Sir James G. Frazer, *The Golden Bough: A Study in Magic and Religion* (abridged ed.; London: Macmillan, 1923).

12. Found in Carl Jung, *The Archetypes and the Collective Unconscious*, trans. R. F. C. Hull ("Bollingen Series" XX [New York: Pantheon Books, 1959]), pp. 149-181.

13. *Ibid.*, pp. 173 ff.

14. *CBC Times*, XIII, No. 45 (May 13-19, 1961), 7.

15. See Mr. Mandel's Preface, no page number.

16. "To the Secret City: From a Winnipeg Sketch-Book," *Queen's Quarterly*, LXI (Summer, 1954), 167-178; "Winnipeg Sketches," *Canadian Forum*, XXXV (November, 1955), 175-176.

Chapter Three

1. Here I quote from a letter written to me by Miss Terry on June 24, 1962.

2. Northrop Frye, "Three Meanings of Symbolism," *Yale French Studies,* IX (1952), 13.

3. "The Influence of Spenser on Yeats," p. 32.

4. *Anatomy of Criticism,* p. 163.

5. *Ibid.,* p. 167.

6. See James Reaney, "An Evening with Babble and Doodle: Presentations of Poetry," *Canadian Literature,* XII (Spring, 1962), 39.

7. *Ibid.,* p. 39.

8. For an informative, penetrating review see Jay Macpherson, *"Listen to the Wind,"* *Canadian Forum,* XLVI (September, 1966), 136-137.

9. See Winnifred Gerin, *Branwell Brontë* (London: Thomas Nelson and Sons Ltd., 1961), p. 206.

Chapter Four

1. See his article "Search for an Undiscovered Alphabet," *Canadian Art,* XCVII (September-October, 1965), 38-41.

Selected Bibliography

The list of primary sources is intended to be complete; secondary items are selected. Within each section of the Bibliography items appear chronologically according to the date of publication or, if unpublished, the date of composition. The following abbreviations are used:

BC   TOYE, WILLIAM (ed.). *A Book of Canada.* London: Collins, 1962.

BP   SCOTT, F. R. & SMITH, A. J. M. (eds.). *The Blasted Pine.* Toronto: Macmillan of Canada, 1957.

CP   DUDEK, LOUIS & LAYTON, IRVING (eds.). *Canadian Poems 1850-1952.* Toronto: Contact Press, 1952.

K   REANEY, JAMES. *The Kildeer & other Plays.* Toronto: Macmillan of Canada, 1962.

OBCV   SMITH, A. J. M. (ed.). *The Oxford Book of Canadian Verse in English and French.* Toronto: Oxford University Press, 1960.

PBCV   GUSTAFSON, RALPH (ed.). *The Penguin Book of Canadian Verse.* Harmondsworth, Middlesex: Penguin Books, 1958.

PMC   WILSON, MILTON (ed.). *Poetry of Mid-Century 1940-1960.* Toronto: McClelland & Stewart, 1964.

RH   REANEY, JAMES. *The Red Heart.* Toronto: McClelland & Stewart, 1949.

PRIMARY SOURCES

I Poems and Books of Poetry

"Quaker Ninth but Roman Eleventh," *Driftwind* (a little magazine published in Cleveland, Fall, 1945), 26.

"Faces and the Drama in a Cup of Tea," *The Undergrad* (1946), 15-18.

"These Wicked Streets," *The Undergrad* (1946), 67-68.

"The School Globe," *The Undergrad* (1946), 31. Also, considerably revised, in *RH*.

"Kodak," *The Undergrad* (1946), 32.

"Miss MacPherson's Letters," *The Undergrad* (1946-47), 36.

"Decadence," *The Undergrad* (1946-47), 39.

"Antichrist as a Child," *The Undergrad* (1946-47), 18. Also, considerably revised, in *RH* and *PMC*.

". . . 1932," *The Undergrad* (1946-47), 26-27.

"The Kites," *The Undergrad* (1946-47), 39. Also, considerably revised, in *RH*.

"The Trojan Horse," *The Undergrad* (1946-47), 58.

"The Orphanage," *The Undergrad* (1946-47), 64.

"Mrs. Wentworth," in *Other Canadians: An Anthology of the New Poetry in Canada 1940-1946*, ed. JOHN SUTHERLAND. Montreal: First Statement Press, 1947, pp. 72-73.

"The Gramophone," *Ibid.*, p. 73.

"Pink and White Hollyhocks," *Contemporary Verse*, XXI (Summer, 1947), 10. Also in *RH*.

"The Death of the Poet," *Contemporary Verse*, XXI (Summer, 1947), 10-11.

"!!Warning!!", *Canadian Poetry Magazine*, XI (September, 1947), 29-30.

"The Birth of Venus," *Here and Now*, I (December, 1947), 72. Also in *PMC*.

"The Death of the Poetess," *Canadian Poetry Magazine*, XI (December, 1947), 29-30. Also in *RH* and *BP*.

"Rewards for Ambitious Trees," *Canadian Poetry Magazine*, XI (December, 1947), 29. Also in *RH* and *PMC*.

"The Rape of the Somnambulist," *Contemporary Verse*, XXIII (Winter, 1947-48), 9-10. Also, in a drastically revised form, in *RH* as "A Fantasy and a Moral."

"Some New Imaginary Conversations and Soliloquies," *The Undergrad* (1948), 13-14. Also in *RH* with the title "A Miscellany."

"The Ivory Steeple," *The Undergrad* (1948), 47. Also in *RH*.

"The Heart and the Sun," *Contemporary Verse*, XXIII (Winter, 1947-48), 11-12. Also, considerably revised, in *RH*.

"Childhood Musette," *Contemporary Verse*, XXIII (Winter, 1947-48), 12. Also, considerably revised, in *RH* as "The Plum Tree."

"The Katzenjammer Kids," *Contemporary Verse*, XXIII (Winter, 1947-48), 13. Also, considerably revised, in *RH*, *OBCV*, *PBCV*, and *PMC*.

"Gray Pillar," *Canadian Forum*, XXVIII (April, 1948), 19. Also in *RH*.

"Klaxon," *Canadian Forum*, XXVIII (April, 1948), 19. Also in *RH*.

"The Dead Rainbow," *Here and Now,* I (May, 1948), 66-68. Part Two of the four parts in *PMC.*

"Green Glass," *Canadian Forum,* XXVIII (May, 1948), 43.

"Night Train," *Canadian Forum,* XXVIII (May, 1948), 42.

"Monologue (Spoken by an orphan servant-girl)," *Canadian Forum,* XXVIII (June, 1948), 67. Also, somewhat revised, in *RH.*

"The Sundogs," *Canadian Forum,* XXVIII (June, 1948), 67. Also, considerably revised, in *RH.*

"Childhood Musette" (a different poem from the one with the same title in *Contemporary Verse,* XXVIII, above), *Northern Review,* II (July-August, 1948), 21.

"The Groats," *Northern Review,* II (July-August, 1948), 22. Also in *RH.*

"The Antiquary," *Northern Review,* II (July-August, 1948), 22.

"The Mysterious Rose-Garden," *Northern Review,* II (July-August, 1948), 23-24.

"A Song for the Suns," *Contemporary Verse,* XXVI (Fall, 1948), 9. Also, considerably revised, in *RH* as "Suns and Planets."

"Madame Moth," *Contemporary Verse,* XXVI (Fall, 1948), 9-10.

"Lake Ontario," *Contemporary Verse,* XXVI (Fall, 1948), 10. Also, slightly revised, in *"The Great Lakes Suite"* in *RH.*

The Red Heart ("Indian File No. 3,"). Toronto: McClelland & Stewart, 1949. Includes the following poems, arranged in four series: *"The Plum Tree"* ("The Plum Tree" [also in *CP*], "The Clouds," "The Sundogs," "Suns and Planets," "The Crow," "Whither Do You Wander?," "The Heart and the Sun," "The Red Heart," "Clouds" [also in *BC*], "The Royal Visit" [also in *BC, BP,* and *PMC*], "Pink and White Hollyhocks," "Gray Pillar," "The Upper Canadian" [also in *The Varsity,* February 5, 1958]); *"The School Globe"* ("Antichrist as a Child" [also in *CP* and *PMC*], "The Two Kites," "The Katzenjammer Kids" [also in *OBCV, PBCV,* and *PMC*], "The Top and the String," "The School Globe," "Scenes for a Stereoscope," "The English Orphan's Monologue," "To My Love," "Dark Lagoon," "The Autobiography of a Marionette"); *"The Great Lakes Suite"* ("Bodies of Fresh Water: Lake Superior, Lake Michigan, Lake Huron, Lake St. Clair, Lake Erie, Lake Ontario" ["Lake Superior," "Lake Huron," and "Lake Erie" also in *BC*], "Grand Bend," "Niagara Falls"); *"The Ivory Steeple"* ("The Ivory Steeple," "The Orphanage," "A Miscellany" [partly reprinted in *The Varsity,* February 5, 1958], "Klaxon," "Rewards for Ambitious Trees" [also in *PMC*], "The Coffins," "The

Groats," "Dream within Dream" [also in *CP*], "The Beauty of
Miss Beatty," "A Fantasy and a Moral," "Coffins," "The Chough"
[also in *OBCV* and *PBCV*], "The Oracular Portcullis" [also in
PBCV], "The Death of the Poetess" [also in *BP*], "A Riddle,"
"The Bird of Paradise").

"The Bird of Paradise," *Northern Review*, II (August-September,
1949), 26. Also in *RH*.

"Winter's Tales," *Contemporary Verse*, XXX (Winter, 1949-50),
3-5.

"Platonic Love," *Contemporary Verse*, XXX (Winter, 1949-50), 5.
Also in *PMC*.

"The Canadian," *Northern Review*, III (December-January, 1949-
50), 45-47.

"To the Avon River Above Stratford, Canada," *Canadian Forum*,
XXX (February, 1951), 255. Also in *Twelve Letters to a Small
Town* (see below) and *PMC*.

"Gunpowder Plot," *Contemporary Verse*, XXXV (Summer, 1951),
17.

"In This Round Place," *Northern Review*, V (October-November,
1951), 20-21.

"The Tall Black Hat," *Canadian Forum*, XXXII (August, 1952), 115.
Also in *PMC*.

"The Table of Dishes," *Northern Review*, VI (April-May, 1953),
27-28.

"The Horn," *Queen's Quarterly*, LXI (Spring, 1954), 102. Also in
OBCV and *PMC*.

"The April and May Eclogues," *The Tamarack Review*, III (Spring,
1957), 31-37. Also in *A Suit of Nettles* (see below).

A Suit of Nettles. Toronto: Macmillan of Canada, 1958. Parts of
this long poem also in *BC*, *OBCV*, and *PMC*.

"Writing & Loving," *The Waterloo Review*, I (Spring, 1958), 17.

"This Page," *The Waterloo Review*, I (Spring, 1958), 18.

"The Man Hunter," in *The Varsity Chapbook*, ed. JOHN ROBERT
COLOMBO. Toronto: The Ryerson Press, 1959.

"The Baby," *Queen's Quarterly*, LXVI (Summer, 1959), 276-279.
Also in *One-man Masque* in *K* (see below).

"A Domestic Song Cycle," *Canadian Forum*, XXXI (August, 1959),
114-116. Also in *Night-blooming Cereus* in *K* (see below).

"A Cellar Song," *Poetry* (Chicago), XCIV (September, 1959), 380.

"The Windyard," *Poetry* (Chicago), XCIV (September, 1959), 381.

"The Thunderstorm," *The Varsity* (January 18, 1960), 5. Also in
Twelve Letters to a Small Town (see below).

"The Dwarf," *The Waterloo Review*, V (Summer, 1960), 26-28. Also
in *One-man Masque* in *K* (see below).

[170]

Selected Bibliography

"The Alphabet," *Alphabet*, I (September, 1960), 30-32.

"To Bishop Berkeley," *The Waterloo Review*, VI (Winter, 1961), 26.

Twelve Letters to a Small Town. Toronto: The Ryerson Press, 1962. From this long poem two parts—"To the Avon River Above Stratford, Canada" and "Town House & Country Mouse" —also in *PMC*.

"A Message to Winnipeg," in *Poetry 62*, ed. ELI MANDEL and JEAN-GUY PILON, pp. 38-47. Excerpt entitled "Le Tombeau de Pierre Falcon" also in *PMC*.

"Rachel." *Canadian Forum*, XLI (March, 1962), 281. Also in *One-man Masque* in *K* (see below) and in *PMC*.

"The Executioner of Mary Stuart," *Canadian Forum*, XLI (May, 1962), 37. Also in *One-man Masque* in *K* (see below).

"Doomsday or the Red-Headed Woodpecker," *Canadian Forum*, XLII (July, 1962), 96. Also in *One-man Masque* in *K* (see below) and in *PMC*.

The Dance of Death at London, Ontario. Drawings by JACK CHAMBERS. London, Ontario: Alphabet Press, 1963.

"Starling with a Split Tongue," *Atlantic Monthly*, CCXIV (November, 1964), 146-147.

"The Stoneboat," in *Quarry Fourteen*, ed. TOM EADIE. Kingston, Ontario: The Quarry Press, 1965, 14-15.

"The Sun," *Atlantic Monthly*, CCXV (February, 1965), 80.

"Gifts," *The Literary Review*, VIII (Summer, 1965), 559.

"The Killdeer," *The Literary Review*, VIII (Summer, 1965), 560-562.

II *Short Stories and Prose Sketches*

"Clay Hole," *The Undergrad* (1946), 15-18.

"The Elevator," *The Undergrad* (1946), 25-26.

"The Book in the Tree," *The Undergrad* (1946-47), 12-13.

"Mr. Whur: A Metamorphosis," *Here and Now*, I (December, 1947), 14-15.

"The Box-Social," *The Undergrad* (1947), 30-31. Also in *New Liberty Magazine*, XXIV (July 19, 1947).

"Afternoon Moon" (first part of a novel, the remainder of which has not been published), *Here and Now*, I (May, 1948), 38-46.

"The Young Necrophiles," *Canadian Forum*, XXVIII (September, 1948), 136-137.

"The Bully," in *Canadian Short Stories*, ed. ROBERT WEAVER and HELEN JAMES. Toronto: Oxford University Press, 1952. Also in *Canadian Short Stories*, ed. ROBERT WEAVER. ("The World's Classics") London: Oxford University Press, 1960.

"Dear Metronome," *Canadian Forum*, XXXII (September, 1952), 134-137.

"To the Secret City: From a Winnipeg Sketch-Book," *Queen's Quarterly*, LXI (Summer, 1954), 167-178.

"Winnipeg Sketches," *Canadian Forum*, XXXV (November, 1955), 175-176.

III   *Articles, Theses, and Related Works*

"Edith Sitwell's Early Poetry or Miss Sitwell's Early Poetry," *The Undergrad* (March, 1948), 28-35.

"The Novels of Ivy Compton-Burnett." Unpublished Master's thesis, University of Toronto, 1949.

"The Novels of Ivy Compton-Burnett," *Canadian Forum*, XXIX (April, 1949), 11-12.

"The Stratford Festival," *Canadian Forum*, XXXIII (August, 1953), 112-113.

"The Plays at Stratford," *Canadian Forum*, XXXIII (September, 1953), 134-135.

"Towards the Last Spike: The Treatment of a Western Subject," *Northern Review*, VII (Summer, 1955), 18-25.

"Another View of the Writers' Conference," *Canadian Forum*, XXXV (October, 1955), 158.

"The Canadian Poet's Predicament," *University of Toronto Quarterly*, XXVI (April, 1957), 284-295. Also in *Masks of Poetry: Canadian Critics on Canadian Verse*, ed. A. J. M. SMITH. Toronto: McClelland & Stewart, 1962.

"The Influence of Spenser on Yeats." Unpublished Ph.D. dissertation, University of Toronto, 1958.

"Isabella Valancy Crawford," in *Our Living Tradition: Second and Third Series*, ed. ROBERT L. McDOUGALL. Toronto: University of Toronto Press, 1959.

"The Canadian Imagination," *Poetry* (Chicago), XCIV (June, 1959), 186-189.

"The Third Eye: Jay Macpherson's *The Boatman*," *Canadian Literature*, II (Winter, 1960), 23-34. Also in *A Choice of Critics: Essays from Canadian Literature*, ed. GEORGE WOODCOCK. Toronto: Oxford University Press, 1966.

"Writing," *Journal of the Royal Architectural Institute of Canada*, XXXVII (April, 1960), 136.

Alphabet: A Semiannual Devoted to the Iconography of the Imagination, ed. JAMES REANEY. 270 Huron Street, London, Ontario: The Alphabet Press. Issue No. 1 published September, 1960; still being published, Number 12 having appeared in August, 1966.

Selected Bibliography

"The Condition of Light: Henry James's *The Sacred Fount*," *University of Toronto Quarterly*, XXXI (January, 1962), 136-151.

"An Evening with Babble and Doodle: Presentations of Poetry," *Canadian Literature*, XII (Spring, 1962), 37-43.

The Boy with an R in His Hand (a book-length tale of the type-riot at William Lyon Mackenzie's printing office in 1826, illustrated by Leo Rampen). Toronto: Macmillan of Canada, 1965.

"Search for an Undiscovered Alphabet," *Canadian Art*, XCII (September-October, 1965), 38-41.

"E. J. Pratt: The Dragonslayer," in *Great Canadians*, ed. PIERRE BERTON and others. Toronto: The Canadian Centennial Publishing Company, 1965.

"Ten Miles High on a Song," *The Globe Magazine* (December 24, 1966), 6-8.

IV   Dramatic Writings and Works for Radio

"Poet and City—Winnipeg" (a half-hour radio program by REANEY as poet and JOHN BECKWITH as composer), "CBC Wednesday Night," September, 1960. Poetic text published later in *Poetry 62* (see above).

The Easter Egg (an unpublished comedy), 1961.

The Revenger's Tragedie by CYRIL TOURNEUR (an adaptation for "CBC Wednesday Night" but never produced and broadcast), February, 1961.

"The Journals and Letters of William Blake" (an unpublished radio talk), "CBC Wednesday Night," April, 1961.

The Killdeer & other plays (The Killdeer, The Sun and the Moon, One-man Masque, Night-blooming Cereus). Toronto: Macmillan of Canada, 1962.

"Wednesday's Child" (an unpublished satirical birthday card for three readers and chamber music ensemble with music by JOHN BECKWITH), "CBC Wednesday Night," December, 1962.

Names and Nicknames (an unpublished children's play), 1963.

The Shivaree (the unpublished libretto of an opera for which JOHN BECKWITH is composing the music), 1965.

Let's Make a Carol: A Play with Music for Children. Story and libretto by REANEY, music by ALFRED KUNZ. Waterloo, Ontario: Waterloo Music Company, 1965.

Part One, Canada Dash, Canada Dot: The Line Across (a Centennial collage of words and music for radio done in collaboration with JOHN BECKWITH), November, 1965, and February, 1966.

Part Two, The Line Up and Down (the second part of the Centennial collage [a third part is planned], to be broadcast in 1967.
Listen to the Wind (an unpublished play in three acts), 1966.

SECONDARY SOURCES

Articles and Selected Reviews

KEE, KENNETH. Review of *RH, The Varsity* (December, 1949), Sees the book as "an important event in Canadian letters."

SUTHERLAND, JOHN. "Canadian Comment," review article on *RH, Northern Review,* III (April-May, 1950), 36-42. Evaluation of the poems in relation to the earlier versions in the little magazines; finds the revisions a weakening.

BROWN, E. K. "Letters in Canada: 1949," review of *RH, University of Toronto Quarterly,* XIX (1950), 262-263. Finds the book uneven, strong in its imagery, trivial in its wit.

PACEY, DESMOND. "The Poetry of the Last Thirty Years," in his *Creative Writing in Canada* (Toronto: The Ryerson Press, 1951), pp. 154-156. Sees the intensely personal *RH* poems as having set Canadian poetry free from the excessive social preoccupation of the 'forties.

COGSWELL, FRED. "Original Technique," review of *A Suit of Nettles, Fredericton Gleaner,* August 11, 1958. Finds Reaney technically the most original modern Canadian poet but lacking in creative ideas.

STOBIE, MARGARET. "Human Frailties and Excellences," review of *A Suit of Nettles, Winnipeg Free Press,* September 20, 1958. Perceptive, appreciative of the book's technical virtuosity and imaginative vigor.

WILSON, MILTON. "Turning New Leaves," review article on *A Suit of Nettles, Canadian Forum,* XXXVIII (October, 1958), 160-162. Very useful; begins the "literary" analysis of the poem.

FRYE, NORTHROP. "Letters in Canada: 1958," review of *A Suit of Nettles, University of Toronto Quarterly,* XXXVIII (July, 1959), 345-348. Very useful: lucid, overall description of the poem dealing briefly with its structure, subject matter, themes, and prosody. Frye says he has never read a book of Canadian poetry with so little "dissociation of sensibility," and that *A Suit of Nettles* succeeds in bringing the highly inarticulate southern Ontario community "into a brilliant imaginative focus."

MANDEL, ELI. Review of *A Suit of Nettles, Dalhousie Review,* XXXIX (Summer, 1959), 262-264. Useful in its intelligent questioning of the poem's overall purpose; sees the form making claims the poem cannot live up to.

AVISON, MARGARET. "Poets in Canada," *Poetry* (Chicago), XCIV (June, 1959), 182-185. Says of *A Suit of Nettles*, it "finds its own way in sublime sureness to that node where the absurd and the dreadful meet."

PONSOT, MARIE. "The Irreducible," review of four volumes, including *A Suit of Nettles, Poetry* (Chicago), XCV (January, 1960), 304-308. Description and high praise; says Reaney's practice of existing forms frees him from what is dead in them.

WINTER, KENNETH. "Cereus Première: Opera of Worth," *Toronto Telegram*, March 26, 1959. Incisive, fairly detailed review of radio première of *Night-blooming Cereus*.

COHEN, NATHAN. "Mr. Reaney Writes a Play," *Toronto Daily Star*, January 14, 1960. Review of stage première of *The Killdeer;* finds it "a desperately bad play" by a talented poet who as yet knows little about playwriting.

WHITTAKER, HERBERT. Review of stage première of *The Killdeer, Globe and Mail* (Toronto), January 14, 1960. Finds Reaney a wild, free spirit in the theater, the play a mixture of good and bad.

MOORE, MAVOR. "This Play May Become Part of Our History," *Toronto Telegram*, January 27, 1960. Review of *The Killdeer;* "likely an historic event—and perhaps even the most important in contemporary Canadian arts and letters."

COLOMBO, JOHN ROBERT. "Antichrist as a Child," *The Varsity*, January 18, 1960, 4-5. A profile interview with Reaney; biographical information.

COULTER, JOHN. "The *Killdeer* and the Fantastic," *Globe and Mail* (Toronto), April 1, 1960. Letter to the editor by another playwright; gets to the essentials of the play better than any of the early reviewers.

KRAGLUND, JOHN. "An Experiment in Lyric Theatre," *Globe and Mail* (Toronto), April 6, 1960. An inept and hostile review of the stage première of *One-man Masque* and *Night-blooming Cereus*.

DUDEK, LOUIS. "Critically Speaking Book Review," CBC Radio, June 10, 1962 (transcript available from: The Director of CBC Information Services, Box 500, Terminal "A," Toronto, Canada). Reviews *Twelve Letters to a Small Town;* sees it as a product of "a divided heart, a colonial Canadian sort of heart."

COGSWELL, FRED. Review of *Twelve Letters, Fiddlehead* (Fall, 1962), 60-61. Praises the clean skill of the writing and the choice of theme.

GRAHAM, KATHLEEN. "This Week I Read," *Leader Post* (Regina), December 8, 1962. Perceptive review of *K*.

WATMOUGH, DAVID. "Critically Speaking Book Review," CBC Radio, December 23, 1962 (transcript available from: The Director of CBC Information Services, Box 500, Terminal "A," Toronto, Canada). Review of *K;* finds *The Killdeer* and *The Sun and the Moon* "superior to the vast majority of current productions in . . . London and New York" and describes Reaney as "one of the most strikingly original voices . . . in contemporary theatre." Useful in its placing of Reaney's dramas in an international context.

WILSON, MILTON. "On Reviewing Reaney," *The Tamarack Review,* XXVI (Winter, 1963), 71-78. Illuminating review of *K* and of *Twelve Letters.*

WILSON, TOM. "Our Nightmare Selves," *Winnipeg Free Press,* January 19, 1963. Review of *K;* effectively answers the criticism that Reaney's plays bear little relation to real life.

LEE, ALVIN A. "A Turn to the Stage: Reaney's Dramatic Verse," *Canadian Literature,* XV-XVI (Winter and Spring, 1963), 40-51; 43-51. Traces development from the *RH* poet to the dramatist.

DARLINGTON, W. A. "In Search of a Roost," *Daily Telegraph* (London, England), May 6, 1963. Review of *K;* finds *The Killdeer* powerful and totally absorbing and suggests a fully professional production at the Edinburgh Festival, The Royal Court, or The Aldwych.

TAIT, MICHAEL. "The Limits of Innocence: James Reaney's Theatre," *Canadian Literature,* XIX (Winter, 1964), 43-48. Attacks *The Killdeer* and *The Easter Egg,* finding them highly unsatisfactory in terms of plausible characterization, coherent action, structure, exposition, unity of style, and in grappling with "the human predicament."

SYLVESTRE, GUY, CONRON, BRANDON and KLINCK, CARL F. (eds.). *Canadian Writers / Ecrivains Canadiens: A Biographical Dictionary.* Toronto: The Ryerson Press, 1964. Biographical account of Reaney and his writings (p. 113).

KLINCK, CARL F. (general ed.). *Literary History of Canada: Canadian Literature in English.* Toronto: University of Toronto Press, 1965. Includes description by MICHAEL TAIT (pp. 648-649) of *The Killdeer* and *The Easter Egg*. Munro Beattie describes briefly *RH* and *A Suit of Nettles* (pp. 787-788).

Lepkin, Benjamin. "The Ring of the Authentic," *Winnipeg Free Press,* June 5, 1965. A review praising *The Boy with an R in His Hand* for its careful research, its lively style, and its elegant typography.

Lee, Alvin A. "Reaney on Stage," *Canadian Forum,* XLVI (September, 1965), 136. Review of the production of *The Sun and the Moon.*

Grieve, Michael. "Magnificent—But Mixup," *Daily Record* (Glasgow, Scotland), September 29, 1965. Review of the Glasgow production of *The Killdeer;* finds it a "stupefying mixture," superb in its characterization, magnificient in its imagery, and doubtful in its message.

Millar, Robins. "A Sordid Whodunit Wrapped in Poetry," *Daily Express* (London, England), September 29, 1965. Finds a rich theme in *The Killdeer* but too much sordidness and melodrama.

A. N. "Enthralling *Killdeer* at Citizens'," *Evening Times* (Glasgow, Scotland), September 29, 1965. Finds *The Killdeer* "an enthralling tale of human emotions."

Wishart, William. "Crime in the Backwoods," *Evening Citizen* (Glasgow, Scotland), September 29, 1965. Finds the play "hardly credible" but imaginative and mystifying.

Wright, Allen. "A Grotesque Triangle in Caricature," *The Scotsman* (Edinburgh, Scotland), September 29, 1965. A moralistic reaction to the "perversions of the mind" depicted in *The Killdeer;* finds the the play entangled in its own complexities.

Spenser, Charles. "The Killdeer," *Financial Times* (London, England), October 1, 1965. Says the play's handling of human passions is in the true manner of myth, an exploration and an illumination of the "hungry gorge of the human heart." Sees Reaney as "a dramatic poet of uncommon and forcible gifts."

Macpherson, Jay. "Listen to the Wind," *Canadian Forum,* XLVI (September, 1966), 136-137. Review of the London, Ontario, production of *Listen to the Wind.* Outlines the main literary sources.

Index

Index

Whitman, Walt, 75
the Whore of Babylon, 125, 127, 143
Wilkin, Jeremy, 13, 119
William, David, 132
Wilson, Milton, 9, 10
wise old man, 43, 44, 46, 125, 135, 141, 156-157
Winchester Geese, 57
Wolfe, James, 85
Wool, Mrs., 141-142

Woolf, Virginia, 118
Wordsworth, William, 161
World War I, 65, 91
World War II, 91-92
Wright, Paul, 114

Yeats, William B., 12-13, 57, 69, 81, 108, 120, 123, 124, 155, 159, 160-161; *Wanderings of Oisin*, 124

Zeno of Citium, 95